SPIRIT ANIMALS

The Wisdom of Nature

Wayne Arthurson

ESCHIA
BOOKS

The Publisher: Eschia Books Inc.

Library and Archives Canada Cataloguing in Publication

Arthurson, Wayne, 1962–
Spirit animals / Wayne Arthurson.

Includes bibliographical references.
ISBN 978-1-926696-21-8

1. Animals—Religious aspects. 2. Totems. 3. Indians of North America—
Mythology. 4. Indians of North America—Religion.
I. Title.

E98.R3A78 2012   299.7'1212   C2012-907089-0

Project Director: Kathy van Denderen
Cover Image: Illustrations were created using elements from
stock photos © Photos.com and © Jupiter Images

Produced with the assistance of the Government of Alberta

Government

We acknowledge the financial support of the Government of Canada.
Nous reconnaissons l'appui financier du gouvernement du Canada.

PC: 38-2

www.eschiabooks.com

To my parents, who guided me.

Contents

Introduction

ANIMALS WERE A VITAL PART of the everyday lives of the indigenous peoples of North America. Native peoples relied on animals for food and to ensure the physical continuation of their society by using the hides, fur and skin for clothing, shelter, footwear and blankets. The bones, horns or shell of an animal could be used to make tools, weapons and medicines. The fat or blubber of the animals was used as food but also as combustion material, lubricant or sealant. Other parts of the animal such as the internal organs could be used to feed a society's dogs—the only domesticated animal before the arrival of the horse—or to make medicines. The skin, teeth, horns or feathers of the animals were sometimes used for ceremonial and spiritual purposes or simply for decoration, to enhance the beauty of the people's lives.

It is not a myth to say that when Native people killed an animal such as a deer or a buffalo, they used every part of the animal. Throwing away or wasting the parts of the animal was considered anathema—something abhorrent and disgraceful. First of all, throwing animal parts away or leaving them to rot had physical consequences. The carcass could attract dangerous predators, such as bears, as well as flies and other insects and animals that carried disease.

But there was another reason why Native peoples used all parts of the animal. The indigenous peoples of North America had a different view of animals than many other peoples in the world. Unlike the Europeans and others who saw animals as separate and lesser entities, Native people saw animals and humans as part of the whole world, and each living being was no better or no worse than the other. Of course, humans did hunt animals for food, hides, furs, medicines and other important materials, but many Native cultures believed that the animals sacrificed themselves so humans could survive, and to waste parts of the animal would be dishonoring that sacrifice.

Native people also believed all animals had spirits or souls. And for the most part, these souls were immortal, the same way human souls were immortal. And when an animal died or was killed, its soul lived on. In some cases, the soul returned to where the animal had lived on the earth. The salmon, for example, would return to the ocean to become another salmon. In other cases, the animal soul moved to a higher plane of existence. But if the animal had been killed and its body and sacrifice had not been treated with the proper respect, the spirit of the animal could stay behind and cause trouble. So certain rituals had to be performed to satisfy the animal's spirit.

Because Native people believed that animals had spirits, over the centuries, they developed descriptions and characterizations of those spirits, which they molded into their stories, their ceremonies and their spirituality. And these rituals were passed down to the following generations who then adapted and changed them so that they became an integral part of their lives, part of their culture.

But the indigenous people of North America didn't create these characterizations and descriptions of the animal spirits out of thin air. In the research and the writing of this book, I sought not only to explore the spiritual, ceremonial and mystical views of animals but also their actual physical attributes. The detailed information on the physicality, behaviors and habitats of these animals have been included to show you, the reader, that by living close to these animals every day for over thousands of years and by observing how they interacted, hunted, ate, bred, lived and died, Native people formed certain perceptions and characterizations of the animals they shared the world with. And it was from these insights that they developed the folklore, the spirituality and attitudes toward these animals and their spirits. From nature and environment comes culture.

It should also be noted that this book is not meant to be read as gospel. It is only a guide, to give an introduction to the significance of animals to Native people and what each animal represented and to see how the meanings behind the animal spirit can be reflected in your own life. And the impressions offered here are not the only interpretations of the animals discussed. Native cultures were diverse, and their views on animals and about many other things in the world varied widely—an animal that some cultures considered important, others did not.

For example, the people of the Pacific Northwest considered fish, more specifically, the salmon, as one of the most important animals in their lives. So salmon played an integral part of their legends and spirituality. Their ceremonies around salmon are specific to their culture. Salmon were seen as immortal creatures that gave up their lives to help humans. But that's because salmon were the primary food source for these people. If there were fewer salmon than previous years, or the runs were late or the fish did not come, then starvation was inevitable. In other cultures where fish were only a small part of a people's diet because their environment was different, these animals had less significance.

Finally, if a connection is made with a certain spirit animal—through your birth date, as a member of that animal clan or for any other reason—the animal spirit is not worshiped the way some other cultures might worship a god or other spiritual being. You *follow* a spirit animal. You can pray to that animal and ask for guidance, but it is done in much the same way that one would pray to, for example, a guardian angel but not to a god.

Also, even though you may follow a particular spirit animal, that doesn't mean you can only connect to that animal and no other. Animals and humans are part of our whole world, and sometimes the deep connections we have with each other are not always evident. Life is also never static; it is ever changing with many nuances. So it is important to have an open mind when reading about the different animal spirits and realize that there are many other meanings. If you are interested in learning more about spirit animals, I encourage you to look at the sources at the back of this book.

In order to get the most understanding of our own existence, we must be open and flexible to all the spirits that exist.

AIR

Crow

CONFUSED SOMETIMES WITH the raven, many Native people see the crow as a great spirit animal. Like the raven, the crow is black, but Native peoples do not see the color black as evil. It is a color of mystery, a color to be explored in order to find out more about life. Truth plays a major role in the definition of the crow spirit. Crows are seen as trickster animals—intelligent but keen to have fun and to get what they want using guile.

This characteristic is not seen as a bad thing. Some of the most important creatures in Aboriginal spirituality and stories are trickster creatures. They are the cultural heroes of many Native peoples in North America.

Crows are similar to ravens, and in some Native cultures and their stories, there is no real difference between the two birds. In other Native groups, both the crow and raven are completely different, even though they may have the same attributes.

The crow is smaller than the raven and is part of the Corvidae family of birds. Crows are believed to have evolved in Central Asia and then progressed into North America and the rest of the world. They are one of the most successful types of birds because they are able to survive in different types of habitats, even living alongside humans in large cities.

Crows are extremely adaptable creatures, eating a wide variety of foods, including insects, smaller birds, fish, fruit and vegetables and carrion. Scavenging for food may have given the crow an evil reputation in places such as Europe, but in North America, Native people saw this attribute as a survival skill.

A crow can count to low numbers, use tools and recognize itself in mirrors and distinguish one human from another by noticing facial features. They are known as observant birds that learn by watching and predicting what will happen next.

The crow's intelligence and observations skills are seen as important traits to many Native groups, and because of this, the bird was featured as a trickser creature in many of their stories.

Others see the crow as a valuable animal that can fly between different worlds and states of being. And with that ability, crows help bring forward certain gifts. The following story is from the Lenape people (also know as "Delaware Indians") of the eastern United States.

The Rainbow Crow

Long ago, before the Lenape lived on the earth, it was always warm and the animals were always happy. But one day, soft snowflakes fell to the ground and covered the earth in white. The world became cold. And even though this was the first time the animals had seen snow, they were not afraid.

But soon the snow kept falling so much that the mouse disappeared under the snow and only the tip of his tail could be seen. Then the rabbit disappeared and only the tops of his ears were visible.

The animals were starting to get worried so they called a council to figure out what to do. They decided they would send someone up to the Kishelamàkänk, the Creator, and ask him to stop the snow.

But who should go, the animals asked.

"We should send the owl," said the opossum. "He is the wisest."

But the other animals thought the owl would get lost in the bright daylight.

"How about the raccoon?" suggested the beaver.

But the animals thought the raccoon would follow its tail instead of its nose and get lost.

"Then the coyote should go," said the skunk. "He is very clever."

But the other animals knew the coyote liked to play tricks and have fun. And he might chase clouds instead.

The snow got deeper and deeper, and the smaller animals climbed on top of the bigger animals so they wouldn't disappear under the snow like the mouse and the rabbit.

"Who should we send?" they wailed in despair.

From the top of a tree came a voice. "I will go," the voice said. The animals looked up and saw it was the rainbow crow, the brightest and most colorful bird of all. The rainbow crow was also smart and could sing beautiful songs in a lovely voice. He was the perfect choice and was sent to find Kishelamàkänk.

The rainbow crow flew high above the earth, past the winds, the clouds, the moon and the stars.

He flew for three days until he reached the home of Kishelamàkänk, but the Creator was too busy to notice him.

The crow sang a beautiful song to the Creator to get his attention.

"What a wonderful gift of a song," the Creator said finally. "Thank you for singing to me. In return, I will give you a gift too. Tell me what you want."

The rainbow crow asked for the Creator to stop the snow from falling.

"I cannot," replied the Creator. "The snow has a spirit of its own. When the snow spirit goes to visit its friend, the wind spirit, it will stop. But it will still be cold."

"Then please make it warm again," said the rainbow crow.

"One day I will. But not for many months."

"But how will I and all the other animals stay warm?" the rainbow crow asked.

"All I can do is give you this." The Creator picked up a long stick and poked it into the sun. The stick caught on fire and gave off great heat. "Fire will keep you warm and will melt the snow so that your friends will be content until warm weather returns.

But I will give this to you only once. Hurry back to earth before the flame goes out."

The rainbow crow began his journey back to earth carrying the fire on the stick. On the first day, sparks from the fire burnt his tail feathers. On the second day, the soot from the burning stick turned all of the rainbow crow's feathers black. On the third day, the fire burned so hot and the stick became so short that the smoke and the ash blew into his mouth. His throat became sore and hoarse. He could only make a "caw caw" sound.

When he arrived on earth at the end of the third day, the snow had reached the tops of the trees, and all the animals had disappeared beneath the snow. The crow flew close to the snow, and the heat of the fire melted it away, releasing his friends.

And so the world received fire, and everyone gave thanks to the rainbow crow, singing songs and dancing all around him. But despite the joyous celebration, the crow was sad. Because he had carried the fire for three days, the smoke had harmed his throat and he could no longer sing wonderful songs; he could only caw. And his beautiful colorful feathers had turned all black.

The Creator heard the crow crying and came down to see what was wrong. He saw how the crow had sacrificed himself to save his friends. He told the crow not to worry.

"Soon, man will come to the earth, and he will become the master of all and take the fire. But not you. You will have freedom. You will never be hurt by man because your meat now tastes like fire and smoke. You will never be captured by man because you no longer have a beautiful voice. And your feathers will have no value because they are black. But in the black of your feathers, all the colors will be seen. Look now and see."

The crow looked at himself and saw tiny rainbows shining in his black feathers. The crow was pleased. And the crow was always free.

In Dakota mythology, the crow is a helper to the Spirit of the South, the being that oversees the summer. This spirit is represented by the plover, a bird that usually lives near bodies of water, running back and forth along the shallows eating insects. In these Dakota stories, the crow and the plover are annually set upon to battle the Spirit of the North and his winter wolves. The wolves always win the battle in the end. But if the two birds use big clubs to beat back the wolves during the annual battle, then the warm weather will last longer that year.

There are also many other Native stories in which the crow plays tricks on humans and other animals or where crows are seen as a warning to others not to be disobedient or disrespectful and to not forget old traditions.

The Magic Pots

A long time ago, an old woman lived in an Ojibwa village. Besides the wigwam she lived in, she also had a separate bark house where she kept five beautiful pots on a shelf. The pots were magical and were not used for cooking or anything else. Instead, the old woman kept the pots in the bark house so the other women of the village could look at them and be inspired to create their own pots. No one could make pottery without the inspiration of the magic pots and, to keep them safe, no one but the old woman was allowed to touch the pots.

One summer, everyone in the village went out at the same time to pick berries, and the old woman went along too. Five young girls were left behind to tend to their chores. After they quickly gathered firewood and completed all of their other chores, the girls got together to play.

Out of curiosity, the girls went to the old woman's bark house where she kept the magic pots so they could see how beautiful they were. But just looking at the pots wasn't enough for them, and they removed the pots from the shelf and took them outside to play, despite the fact that the old woman had forbidden anyone to touch the pots.

As the girls were playing, a wolf appeared. The girls were frightened and ran into one of the houses to get away from the wolf. Suddenly, they heard a noise like thunder, and the wolf disappeared. When the girls came out of the house, they found all of the pots shattered into tiny pieces.

When the old woman returned home from berrypicking, she found out what had happened. She went to the five girls, and they admitted to breaking the pots. As soon as they did, the disobedient girls changed into five black crows that flew away cawing.

Without the magic pots, the women of the village no longer knew how to make pottery, and that is why the Ojibwa no longer make pots. But the crows live on, and in summer you can see them in tall trees, uttering a mournful caw, caw.

The Crow People

In an interesting parallel to the survival and adaptation ability of the crow comes the story of the people who were named after this black bird. Calling themselves the Apsaalooke, these people lived in the valley of the Yellowstone River, from Wyoming through Montana and into North Dakota. The Apsaalooke were called the Crow people by other tribes in the area, and the name still remains today.

For a long time, the crow people battled the Blackfoot, the Gros Venture, the Pawnee, the Assiniboine and the Sioux, among others. It is believed that the Crow people originally lived farther east but were pushed west by the larger and stronger Sioux, who were their longtime enemies.

When the Europeans came, the Crow people allied themselves with the white man, mostly because the white man also battled against the Sioux and other nations.

But the Crow people didn't ally with the Europeans because of petty political differences. In 1848, a boy named Aleek-chea-ahoosh was born to the Crow people. During his childhood, almost 90 percent of his people had been killed because they contracted smallpox, a disease that the Europeans brought with them to North America.

When Aleek-chea-ahoosh became a man by completing certain rights of passage, he was given another name: Alaxchiiaahush. In English, this was translated to "Plenty Coups," which meant he had undertaken and succeeded in several acts of bravery.

Plenty Coups eventually became the chief of his people and was one of the most visionary men of his time. Alaxchiiaahush was also known for his visions, in which he saw the future of his people.

He was one of few Natives who predicted that the Europeans would become the dominant culture in North America. And he saw that if his people wanted to survive and continue with their culture, they would have to adapt.

Alaxchiiaahush also had a vision in which the buffalo disappeared and were replaced on the plains by a strangely similar creature, an animal with a spotted hide. That vision came true when the buffalo were eradicated and cattle became prevalent.

As a result of the visions Alaxchiiaahush experienced, the Crow people allied themselves with the Europeans. The chief saw this alliance as the only way for his people to keep their traditions intact amid the major changes taking place in North America at that time.

Alaxchiiaahush's ideas did work—to some extent. When the U.S. Congress was planning to abolish the Crow nation and take away their land, Alaxchiiaahush traveled to Washington, DC, to plead for this people. He made several trips to speak to Congress from 1888 to 1898, and in the end, he managed to save his people and 80 percent of their traditional lands.

Although the Crow people suffered like many other Native peoples as the result of the expansion of European culture and the influx of white people, they managed to keep control of much of their ancestral land despite Europeans wanting the land for mining and taking other natural resources. The Blackfoot and the Sioux, among other Native groups, were forcibly removed from their traditional lands and placed on reserves far away.

One of Alaxchiiaahush's most memorable quotes is this: "Education is your most powerful weapon. With education, you are the white man's equal; without education, you are his victim, and so shall remain all your lives."

So, like the bird from which they were called, the Crow people showed adaptability to a difficult situation and managed to survive. They were able to keep their land and pass on their traditional culture in an ever-changing world.

Finding the Crow

There are a number of crow clans in North America, including the Chippewa, the Menominee, the Caddo, the Tlingit and many other groups in the southwestern United States.

If you follow the crow as a spirit animal or if you are of the crow clan, you are a seeker of truth—someone who understands what is really going on and can point out the truth to others who cannot see it. Justice plays a major role in the life of a crow.

You are able to travel easily between the material and spiritual worlds and can bring back messages to others who do not have that gift. Crows also can see magic in the material world and teach others to see a situation in a different light.

Because flocks of crows always appoint a lookout when they are feeding to warn of danger, people of the crow are bellwethers. They can foresee when change is coming and through their actions are able to affect that change.

Crows are keen on taking up new projects and challenges, though sometimes they may take on too many at one time.

If you encounter a crow or feel the need to follow one, there may be a major shift taking place in your life, and you must be willing and ready to accept that change. The change can be good, or as the Crow people have shown, it can be a difficult adjustment where action must be taken. However, if you adapt, you will survive and push through.

Because the crow is seen as a trickster, the appearance of this bird in your life might mean that you are about to be tricked or conned, so be on your guard. Or perhaps you are getting signs from other spirits, but you haven't been able to determine the meaning of these signs or where this guidance is coming from. The crow's appearance in your life should help you discover the truth.

One of the best ways to call the crow spirit into your life is to be observant of your surroundings. Be aware of the good and bad in your life while quietly searching for the truth. Being open to change and willing to adapt to whatever comes your way will reveal the wisdom of the crow spirit.

Also, try to distinguish between the crow and the raven animal spirits. While these animals are similar in appearance, their messages can be quite different (see the section on Raven).

Eagle

IN MOST NATIVE CULTURES, the eagle is considered one of the great spirit animals. Almost every Native group from the north to the south and from the east to the west honors the eagle.

Eagles are stately birds of prey that can soar higher above the earth than any other bird. And because eagles can catch prey in mid-flight, this ability only adds to the seemingly magical qualities of these birds.

Of course, other birds of prey hunt in this way, but because eagles are one of the largest of such birds, with a large wingspan depending on the species, they are treated with more respect than falcons and hawks. Eagles have large heads and thick beaks, and when they are perched on a tree branch or the top of a tree, their stance is erect, giving them a regal appearance.

There are many species of eagles found on every continent save for Antarctica. Overall though, there are four basic groups: fish eagles, booted eagles, snake eagles and giant forest eagles. The most common and prominent eagle in North America is the bald eagle, of the fish group, and the golden eagle, which is a booted eagle.

Bald eagles live only in North America. Known for its brown body and white head, this eagle is a large raptor; it weighs about 15 pounds with a wingspan of up to eight feet. It mostly hunts fish and lives near rivers, lakes, sea coasts and other bodies of water that have an abundance of fish. However, this eagle also hunts a wide variety of mammals and other birds, including raccoons, rabbits, beavers, muskrats, ducks, gulls, grebes, egrets and even deer fawn and great horned owls. Bald eagles have been known to successfully hunt Canada geese in mid-air. They also eat crabs, reptiles and amphibians. Bald eagles are not adverse to carrion, which can be their main source of food during the winter months.

A bald eagle nest averages a depth of 13 feet, is 8.2 feet wide and can weigh around one ton, the largest nest of any bird in North America. Bald eagles take about five years to become sexually mature and can live up to 20 to 25 years. An interesting aspect of bald eagles is that they are monogamous and mate for life.

The population of bald eagles was around 300,000 in the 1800s. However, because of hunting and the use of DDT, the population plummeted to about 400 mating pairs by 1950. Their population was higher in Canada and Alaska, but the numbers were low enough for the bird to be considered endangered.

Stringent hunting laws and the all-out ban of DDT allowed the population of bald eagles to increase to more than 100,000 in 1995, and bald eagles were reclassified as a "threatened species." In 2007, the classification was removed.

Many Native peoples consider the eagle the chief of the birds because of its hunting ability and courage to fly higher than all other birds. They soar high above the landscape and observe the world from their lofty heights. Because many Native cultures believe the Creator lives high in the sky and sees all from above, eagles are seen as deeply connected to the Creator.

The eagle is an intermediating spirit between the material world and the spirit world, and between humans and the Creator. Therefore, their animal spirit was called upon time and time again to communicate with other spirits or to convey prayers, offerings and thanks from humans to the Creator.

There are several ceremonies, songs and dances that call or invoke the spirit of the eagle. For example, the people of the Pacific Northwest brush the ground and the floor of lodges with the down of an eagle before ceremonies or potlatches as sign of respect, peace and welcoming.

In Sun Dance ceremonies performed by Plains cultures, such as the Blackfoot, the eagle is represented in a variety of ways. For example, a whistle made from the bone of an eagle is used to make music during special dances. A fork in the lodge where the dance is held represents the eagle nest. And a shaman will use an eagle feather fan to heal those who are present. During the dance, the center pole in the lodge is touched with the eagle feather and then briefly placed on the person or people who require healing. The eagle fan is then held to the sky, asking for the power of the eagle to carry the prayers of the people to the Creator.

Eagle feathers are one of the most prized totems in most Native communities. Finding an eagle feather is considered a sacred event in someone's life. For many, it is a sign of great fortune or a sign that the finder has been blessed by the Creator because the person has succeeded in some great accomplishment. In some cultures, only the chief was allowed to possess an eagle feather, and if someone found an eagle feather, it meant that person was in line to be a great leader.

Other Native groups did not have the stipulation that only chiefs were allowed to have eagle feathers, and almost everything the people carried or wore, such as regalia, fans, bustles and headdresses, was adorned with eagle feathers that they found. These types of items were seen as a sign of luck, honor and achievement.

Although finding an eagle feather is considered a wonderful fortune to the person who finds it, if he gives that feather to someone else, he is showing respect and honor to the recipient. In some cultures, it is customary for a person to give a feather to an elder they admire or to a person who has done great things for the people.

Because eagles are known to be excellent hunters, many Plains people gave eagle feathers to courageous warriors. The warriors attached the feathers to their weapons, clothing or headdress. The more eagle feathers a warrior had, the nobler the warrior. Even today, some Native peoples offer eagle feathers to individuals who have shown greatness.

The following story explains one reason why eagle feathers are respected and why the bird's animal spirit is held in high esteem.

The Eagle and the Linnet

A long time ago, the birds were discussing which of them was the best flyer.

"I'm the fastest flyer," said the hummingbird. "I dash about back and forth between all the other birds so I'm the best flyer."

"No, I'm the best," said the duck. "Every winter I fly for weeks at a time to get away from winter. So I'm the best flyer."

"Ha. None of you can fly in the dark like me," said the owl. "So I'm the best flyer."

Then all the other birds joined in the argument, saying they were the best flyer.

When the argument ended much later, the linnet, a small dull bird that lived in the bushes, had an idea. "We should have a race. The bird that flies the highest in the sky will be named the best flyer."

The other birds were unsure what to think about the linnet's idea. The linnet was known to be a bit of a trickster, but they didn't know why he suggested such a race. The linnet was quick, but he couldn't fly high.

The birds decided to go through with the linnet's idea and set the race for the next day.

When the sun came up in the morning, all the birds gathered for the start of the race—all of them except the linnet. But the birds were so excited they didn't notice the linnet was missing.

When the race began, the faster birds flew away quickly. The hummingbird was the fastest and soon led the race. But the hummingbird started to get tired, and when he couldn't fly any higher, he dropped out of the race. Many of the other faster birds also soon tired and abandoned the race.

The owl was slower, but he passed the hummingbird and took the lead. But then the owl looked down and saw how high he was. He was used to flying low to the ground so he became afraid. The owl decided to quit the race and headed back to the forest.

The duck flew strong and hard, passing the hummingbird and the owl as well as the other birds as they descended from the sky. Soon the duck was at the front. But the duck didn't like to climb that high. Although he was strong, he usually only flew in a straight line when the ducks flew south for the winter. He decided enough was enough and gave up.

Only the hawk, the falcon and the eagle were still in the race. After a while, the falcon and then the hawk couldn't fly any higher. The eagle, with his long, strong wings, flew the highest. He seemed to touch the sky as he flew.

But before the eagle decided to turn back and claim victory, he felt something stirring in his back feathers. It was the linnet. The bird had hitched a ride on the eagle and was flying slightly higher than the eagle.

The linnet suddenly turned and flew quickly to the ground, much to the amazement of the other birds that waited there to see who the winner would be.

"I fly the highest," the linnet said. "So I am the best flyer."

It was true; it seemed as though the linnet had flown higher than the eagle. But the other birds could not understand how the linnet had flown so high for such a small bird.

When the eagle finally soared to the ground, he told the other birds what the linnet had done.

"That makes no difference," said the linnet. "We agreed that the bird that went the highest in the sky was the best flyer. And I went highest in the sky. So I win."

But the other birds didn't agree. The eagle had flown the highest, showing bravery by almost touching the sky. And since he had to carry another bird on his back, the eagle was deemed the strongest of the birds. So all the birds honored the eagle.

And to this day, bravery and strength is honored with the gift of an eagle feather.

Native people do not encourage obtaining eagle feathers through hunting the bird. As noted earlier, the feathers are meant to be found or given as a gift by someone else.

However, in some cultures, young warriors proved their bravery and ingenuity by climbing high to the nests of eagles or to where they perched and tried to snatch a feather from the body of a live eagle. They did this without harming the eagle or any of its offspring if they were in the nest.

Under United States law, only individuals who are certified members of a federally recognized tribe are allowed to obtain eagle feathers, and the feathers are to be used only for religious and spiritual purposes.

The majority of Native cultures consider it taboo to kill an eagle. Killing an eagle by accident or by hunting one will not only bring harm to the individual but could also bring harm and bad luck to an the entire tribe, as is shown in the following story.

The Stranger

Once there was a Native hunter out in the mountains. It was nighttime and he was resting in a hunting lodge after a long day at the hunt. He was pleased with himself because he had killed a large deer that day. The deer meat was hanging outside his lodge. Sometime during the night, a loud whooshing noise outside the lodge woke the hunter up. It sounded like a quick wind had blown past.

The hunter went outside to check what was going on and saw an eagle. The eagle was tearing at the deer that the hunter had caught. Angry, the hunter shot the eagle and went back inside the lodge to sleep.

When he returned to his village the next day, he showed his people the deer he had killed and told the story of how he had hunted it down. He did not say anything about the eagle he had killed. If he had told them about killing the eagle, the people would need to do an special eagle dance to apologize to the eagle spirit. And the hunter would have to leave some of the deer meat outside for the family of the eagle to make up for the death of their brother.

The hunter was greedy and wanted all the meat for his people. He remained quiet about what he had done.

The people had a feast to celebrate the wonderful deer the hunter had killed. While the celebration was taking place around the fire, a stranger showed up and asked if he could join in the feast. Because the stranger was not armed and did not pose any threat, the people welcomed him as a guest.

Later in the evening, the stranger asked about the deer, noting that it looked like it had some marks of an eagle's beak tearing into the flesh. The hunter said he never saw any marks. Nor did he see any eagles during his hunt he added.

The stranger nodded, stood up and then began a strange dance. At the end of his dance, he jumped in the air, giving a sharp shout when he landed. As soon as he did this, one of the elders in the group instantly died, which shocked everyone.

"Are you sure you didn't see an eagle during your hunt?" the stranger asked the hunter.

"I did not," replied the hunter.

So the stranger danced again. And again, when he shouted and landed, another person died instantly. The people were so afraid that they could not move to run away.

Again the stranger asked the hunter about the eagle. And again the hunter denied seeing an eagle.

Seven people died before the hunter finally admitted what he had done. He had not only seen the eagle, but he also had killed it he told the group.

The stranger didn't dance anymore. He told the people that they had to do an eagle dance to apologize for killing the eagle. And after the people finished the dance, the stranger showed them where to take some of the deer meat for the eagle's family.

When the people placed the meat on the ground, the stranger turned into an eagle and flew away. The people then realized that the stranger was actually the brother to the eagle that had been killed. They learned from this experience to never hunt an eagle. And if someone from their tribe accidentally killed an eagle, the people performed the eagle dance to ask for forgiveness for what they had done.

Finding the Eagle

As noted earlier, the eagle is one of the most honored and respected of all the spirit animals. Native cultures across the continent revere these regal birds as animals with special powers. The various representations of the eagle animal spirit include spiritual protection, strength, courage, leadership, creation, healing, carrying of prayers, a close connection to the Creator and intimate knowledge of magic.

Because eagles soar above the world, looking down on all that is there to see, they can see hidden truths and the overall pattern of the world. Eagles are also strong flyers with keen eyesight, graceful strength and power that is balanced with intuition. Their animal spirit is connected with esteemed leaders, teachers and spirit guides.

And because eagles build massive nests and are fiercely protective of their young, some people, such as the Pawnee in Oklahoma, consider the birds to be a symbol of family and fertility.

Eagles are also one of the most widespread clan animals used by Native cultures. There are too many groups to list here, but a few Native cultures that have eagle clans include the Tlingit, the Haida, the Osage, the Caddo, the Cherokee and the Anishinaabe. Eagle clans are present throughout North America.

If you are a member of an eagle clan or follow the eagle as a spirit animal, you are a born leader, charismatic and able to endure difficult challenges and tasks because you have tremendous confidence in yourself.

You are the kind of person who doesn't waste much energy but acts quickly and decisively when the need arises. You have healing talents, an intuition that can sense underlying meanings and the ability to analyze a situation. You see the whole picture rather than just the individual parts of it.

Soaring above the material world and easily connecting with the spirit world—not just to help yourself but to offer guidance and healing to others who need it—is another aspect of someone with an eagle spirit.

If you encounter an eagle, either physically or spiritually, it can symbolize many things. Eagles are the apex predator of the sky so they are associated with communication and deep thought. An eagle animal spirit also symbolizes reinvention, either by a cleansing to renew yourself or by embarking on a new path or task. There could be an imminent opportunity, a change or some idea you are considering, and the appearance of the eagle signifies that you should act quickly to take advantage of the situation.

If you are connected to the eagle spirit, it's a time for creative inspiration, which could lead to a spiritual awakening that will give you a much broader awareness and connection to the spiritual world.

You can call on the eagle when you are caught up in the mundane details of life and need to expand your awareness. Or perhaps you are in a moment of transition or undergoing some kind of struggle. The eagle can help when you have to make a major decision but can't seem to figure out which way to turn.

Calling on the eagle can be as simple as using its feathers in a ceremony, during meditation or in a dance or prayer that you use to express spirituality or awareness. However, as stated earlier, eagle feathers are sacred and must be earned. You must find an eagle feather or be given one as a gift. Or your must do as the warriors used to do and stalk an eagle and pull a feather from its plumage without harming the bird. You also must be careful when receiving or purchasing an eagle feather because there is much fraud in the sale of eagle feathers. What is called an "eagle" feather could actually be from a crow, magpie or other bird.

You should also be aware that the eagle spirit does not simply show up when you call. Most other spirit animals don't either, but a longer waiting period is required for the eagle. Perform the ceremonies, dances, songs, prayers or meditation regularly, but be patient. Trying to rush the arrival of the eagle spirit will not result in success. It may, in fact, lengthen the waiting process.

You can also take notice whether you have judged someone recently. Write about these memories to become more aware of them. Also write down events for which you are grateful. Both of these tasks may help to evoke the eagle spirit. And going to a place high above the ground, whether it be in nature—such as a cliff, the top of a mountain or valley—or a humanmade place such as a bridge or a tall building, may also help you become closer to the eagle spirit. Once you are at this high place, look down, without judgment, at all that you observe. Breathe deeply as you do this, and do not close your eyes. These techniques will not necessarily hasten the arrival of an eagle spirit, but they may open something in you that will bring the eagle closer.

Those people who connect with the eagle spirit may exhibit some aspects of this majestic bird's power, but you must respect that power and not be prideful or disdain others if they follow different spirit animals that may seem to have less authority. To behave in this manner is not in the eagle's nature.

Owl

To be honest, few people follow the owl as an animal spirit. And the reason for this is quite simple: in several Native cultures, the owl is considered an omen of death or is a warning of evil behavior. For example, according to the Cherokee people, if an owl flies over you in daylight, it is an omen of bad luck, even death. To some people, hearing the sound of an owl at night is considered an unlucky omen. It can be a message of evil, a future accident, a coming sickness or the arrival of death.

Most European cultures see owls as a wise creature as do some Native cultures. But while Europeans view the owl as a benevolent creature, some Native groups see the owl using its wisdom for evil.

Or at the very least for negative purposes that are not entirely evil.

Among the Hocagara people of Wisconsin, if a warrior is killed within the sanctuary of the chief's lodge, an owl would appear to them before the incident occurred. The owl would speak as a human, saying that the warrior or the warrior's people would have misfortune. And that could mean the demise of the people or the nation who committed the crime.

It is said that one winter in the 1830s, Glory of the Morning, the first female chief of the Hocagara people, was walking in the pine woods near her home when she heard an owl's cry.

Glory of the Morning, or Hopokoekau, was born around 1709, the daughter of the chief of the Hocagara people, who lived in the area now called Wisconsin. She lived for almost 100 years, a long time for those days. As chief, she allied her people with French fur traders and fought battles against other nations that had harassed the Hocagara people for years.

According to Hocagara lore, as she was walking through the pine forest near her home, an owl called out. She heard the sound as though someone was calling her name. Hopokoekau returned home, wrapped herself in furs on her bed and died peacefully that same night. It is also said that on the night she died, a severe blizzard occurred, the like of which had never been seen for a long time. And during that blizzard, the sound of thunder was heard, a rare occurrence during winter.

For the most part, almost all 200 species of owl are nocturnal animals that are quite active during twilight and dawn. And all have a keen sense of sight and hearing, along with the ability to turn their head almost completely around. Owls have large eyes, at least compared to the size of their bodies. Owls are birds of prey—carnivores that hunt other animals—with ears and eyes at the front of their head, rather than at the side like some other birds.

Owls rely on stealth and surprise to capture their prey. Most have a dull color that makes them practically invisible at night. Owls also have serrations on their feathers, especially those at the edges of their wings, that enable them to fly silently. They can fly and flap their wings in silence while stalking their prey. The only owls that don't have this adaptation are the ones that hunt fish, and thus don't need it.

The owl's ability to see at night and hunt silently and successfully in darkness where humans could not see them was the reason many Native cultures gave evil connotations to the bird. The medicine of the owl was considered powerful and had to be respected, even feared. This belief is reflected in the following story from the Kalmath people in Oregon.

The Medicine of the Owl

In the beginning, the Creator made all the world and the animals that lived in it, including the bird people. But there was an evil spirit who wanted to show that he had the same power as the Creator, so he created another kind of bird. This bird was only seen at night, and no one heard its voice because it could not sing. It was a deadly hunter that could fly without making a noise. But the owl lived and hunted alone—no one ever saw this bird with any other birds.

And so it happened that whenever one of the people went on a vision quest to ask the Creator for guidance, this nocturnal bird was the first image to appear to them.

The bird tried to convince the people to use its power instead of the Creator's. "Look at me," said the owl. "I fly silently so no one can hear me coming. My claws can kill any animal so I am a successful hunter and warrior. My eyes are wide and round like the sun so I can see everything. Nothing can hide from me—nothing in the present, the past or the future. I have great power, so if you really want to help yourself, take my power and be strong."

Although the owl's medicine was tempting, most people refused the owl. But there was one man who took the owl's power. He became powerful, and everyone was afraid of him. If the people did not listen to him or did not do what they were told to do, the man used his power against them.

Some people offered gifts to the man so he would agree to use his owl powers against someone they had a disagreement with or people they did not like. The owl man killed or hurt those people.

The people grew more afraid of the owl man. And to seek guidance on how to deal with him, they held a sweat lodge. They called to the Creator to help them battle the owl. To help the people, the Creator sent the coyote and the raven to fight the owl. A vicious battle ensued, but the coyote and the raven were victorious. The owl was defeated.

This story from the Kalmath people tells us that if you fear the owl and what he brings, calling on the coyote and the raven will help dismiss that fear. It also tells us that if the owl calls out to us, danger or even death may be coming. The owl calling out to you may be a warning, but if you change your ways, pay attention or improve something in your life, then you can avoid danger and death.

This brings up another aspect of owl as a spirit animal. Although some people view an owl as a harbinger of death, this doesn't mean it is an evil creature. Death is just another part of life, probably one of the biggest mysteries of life. And the owl, if one believes it is connected to death, means that this bird may have knowledge of this mystery. So an owl's medicine, though considered powerful and possibly evil by some, can be used to seek knowledge that most people are afraid to search for because they believe that knowledge could be dangerous.

In other Native cultures, the owl isn't viewed as a sign of death nor a wise and friendly creature but rather a bogeyman, sometimes called Big Owl. In some stories, the owl figure is used to warn children to behave and not cry at night and to listen to their parents. Some cultures such as the Tlingit respect the owl as a skilled hunter and warrior, and the warriors would mimic the owl's cry as they ran into battle. The warriors called upon the owl's spirit to give them strength and to strike fear into the hearts of their enemies.

And in some other cultures, the owl is considered quite harmless. Instead of symbolizing death and darkness, the owl is a bumbling or vain creature that was punished by the Creator for being vain or selfish or for not listening.

According to the Montagnais people of Quebec, there was once a great owl, the largest owl in the world. It had a loud call that it was proud of. But when the owl tried to imitate the roar of a waterfall, the Creator thought the owl was becoming too proud, so he shrunk the owl to the size of a tiny bird with a weak voice, like the sound of dripping water. This is the Northern Saw-Whet owl, which is only 7 to 9 inches in length and makes a quiet whistling sound.

And there is this story from the Iroquois people.

Why the Owl Has Big Eyes

A long time ago when the world was being made, the Everything-Maker, Raweno, was busy creating all the animals, the plants, the rocks, the forest, the lakes, the rivers, the mountains and all the things that cover the earth.

Raweno was in the process of making the owl but was not finished. The owl had a head, two eyes, a body, strong wings and a voice. The owl was impatient and wanted his body to be finished, so as Raweno was working, the owl kept talking.

"I want a long neck like the swan," the owl demanded. "And red feathers like the cardinal and a beak like the hawk."

"Yes, yes. Whatever you like. But you must wait your turn," said Raweno. "And you must close your eyes. You know that no one is allowed to watch me work. Turn around and close your eyes. I am busy creating the rabbit right now."

Raweno then turned to the rabbit and said, "What would you like, Rabbit?"

"I want long legs and ears. And fangs. Can I have fangs?" asked the rabbit. "And claws. Can I have claws?"

"Sure, I think we can give you some claws and fangs," said the Everything-Maker, patting the rabbit's new long ears.

"Silly Rabbit. You should ask for wisdom—that's something you can really use!" shouted the owl.

"This is your last warning, Owl!" shouted Raweno. "Be quiet and wait your turn."

The owl turned to look at Raweno. "You have to give us what we ask for," he hooted. "You have to, and I demand wisdom."

"You were warned, Owl!" shouted Raweno. He pushed the owl's head down into his body, which made the owl's neck disappear. He then shook the bird roughly, which made the owl's eyes widen in fright. He then pulled on the owl's ears until they stuck out from his head.

Raweno snapped his fingers. "There you go, Owl. I have made your ears big, so you can listen better. I have made your eyes big, so you can see better. I have made your neck shorter, so you can hold up your head easier. And your head is packed with wisdom as you have requested. Now use that wisdom and fly away before I take everything away."

Since the owl now had wisdom, he was no longer foolish. He flew quickly away, pouting and hooting.

Raweno turned around to finish his work on the rabbit and said, "Okay, Rabbit, you want claws and fangs, is that right?"

But the rabbit was nowhere to be seen. The commotion with the owl had frightened the rabbit and he had hopped away from the scene in fear, too afraid to wait for his fangs and claws.

The owl, in his wisdom, knew that if he angered Raweno, he would have lost everything. So he only comes out at night, when Raweno is asleep.

As for timid Rabbit, he knows his claws and fangs are waiting for him, but he is too afraid to go back and ask for them.

Finding the Owl

For the most part, people do not seek the owl as an animal spirit because of its connotation with evil and death. However, some clans do follow the owl, and these clans are mostly in the southern U.S. There are also owl carvings on totem poles in the Pacific Northwest.

But there are those who lean toward the darkness, and this is not always for evil purposes. People who seek or follow the owl tend to be interested in the unknown and mystery. They like to explore the different levels of existence. There is wisdom to be gained as one follows the owl with logic and reason, as well as a desire to investigate or delve deeper into ideas that don't make sense or are fantastical.

People connected to the owl animal spirit tend to want to uncover the motivations of people. Other people are keen to share their secrets. Owls are also, supposedly, adept at the art of seduction.

The owl is a sign on the Native American zodiac representing those born between November 23 and December 21. People born under this sign are usually artists, writers, teachers and conservationists. Little is said in the Native American zodiac about the dark side of the owl save for the fact that they may be reckless because they act too quickly. In the real world, however, owls are known to be birds that fly quite slowly.

If you encounter an owl, do not be afraid. The owl can be an omen of death but not always. Only if you hear the owl call you personally can it mean an impending death. But it does not necessarily mean you will die; it could be a warning of danger ahead, and if you pay attention, you can avoid the threat.

And death does not always signify the death of the body but could mean the death of a lifestyle or a way of doing things. The appearance of an owl can indicate a major change is coming, one that has the potential to transform you into a different person with an entirely different view on life. So in many cases, the owl can represent rebirth after a major life-changing event.

Another meaning associated with an owl's appearance has to do with deception by others, but if you pay attention, you should be able to see through their guile. The animal spirit of the owl can also mean that your creative energies are better used at night, and adjusting your daily rhythm could be in order.

Some people will call on the owl for other, though not immoral, reasons. You can call on the owl when you need to make a decision that, no matter what you choose, will change your life drastically—what you were in the past will be gone, and you will be reborn.

Because owls can see in the darkness, they are often called upon to help you see your way forward when the future is dark and you need guidance.

An owl is also helpful to call upon when you wish to discover the hidden talents or skills in yourself and in others. And once the owl appears, you will be able to bring forth light to help yourself as well as loved ones.

One of the ways to call on the owl is to change your daily routine for a while. Spend more time in the night and get comfortable with the darkness. It may be difficult to see at night, and at times, it can seem almost lifeless. But the night is just as alive as the daytime. There is nothing inherently wrong with the darkness; night is just part of the daily cycle of life.

Although many Native cultures interpreted the owl as an animal of the night, the dark and possibly death, for the most part, the bird was not viewed as an "evil" animal. No animal was considered inherently evil—each is a natural part of the earth. And whatever some may have thought, they knew deep down that the owl was a splendid hunter and warrior. And for a lot of Native peoples, these skills were a great medicine indeed.

Raven

THE RAVEN IS A FASCINATING spirit animal. Because of its dark color, it is connected to darkness and the night. The raven feeds on carrion, which is why the bird is sometimes also associated with death. And because of the bird's intelligence and survival skills, it can also evoke themes of creation, the trickster spirit and selfishness.

It is the intelligence of ravens, especially when compared to other birds, that is reflected in Native spirituality and stories. Many Native cultures don't distinguish between the crow and the raven in their stories, even though the birds are different (see Crow chapter).

Ravens are the largest of the Corvidae family (which includes the magpie, the blue jay, the crow and other similar birds) weighing 1.5 to 4.4 pounds and standing 22 to 30 inches tall. They have a wing-span of 40 to 59 inches. Crows are much smaller birds. Both animals are social with a tendency to flock, but ravens normally live as a mating pair. And though ravens do live near humans and in large urban centers, they prefer to live in wilderness areas.

The sound a raven makes is similar to the caw of a crow but is deeper because of the raven's larger size. Sometimes the raven makes a sound like a throaty goose call. But the bird makes other noises as well, such as gurgles and knocking sounds, whereas crows do not make these sounds. At least 30 different types of raven vocalizations have been recorded.

And because they are bigger with a longer wing-span, ravens soar more than crows, who rarely soar at all. Ravens are more widely distributed than crows and are found throughout the entire North-ern Hemisphere, surviving quite well in the Arctic all the way through the boreal forest and the Pacific rain forest across to the Atlantic coast all the way down into Central America.

Ravens are omnivorous, eating almost anything, including carrion. Although Europeans and other peoples saw the bird's diet of carrion as a harbinger of death and darkness, Native people saw it differ-ently. Other seemingly more majestic animals such as the bear and the bald eagle also eat carrion, so the crow and raven are no different or worse than those animals.

In fact, no Native culture in North America sees the crow or raven as a symbol or sign of death. The raven and crow are signs of good fortune, possibly because of their ability to survive and because they have no natural predators. One reason other animals don't prey on ravens is because these birds viciously defend their young when attacked, using their large beaks and sometimes dropping stones on the attackers.

Native people noticed these behaviors as well as the intelligence behind the bird's dark eyes. In many of the stories about ravens, their intelligence is a major feature. Some stories depict them as tricksters, but for many Native people, the trickster character isn't evil. He is seen as more of a cultural hero—a fun-loving, sometimes selfish creature that occasionally causes trouble for others. A raven's ability to survive in almost any environment, along with its "playfulness," seems to reflect some human-like traits. Ravens are one of the few birds that seem to "play." These are some of the reasons why ravens are considered strong medicine and sacred animals.

In the Tlingit culture on the Pacific Coast, the raven is featured as two separate but similar characters. One raven is a positive spirit that creates and heals the world and is responsible for giving gifts to humanity. The other raven character is more childish, sneaky and selfish. But there is not always a distinction between the two creatures, and it's not always apparent which version of the raven is being talked about. The Inuit and the Aleuts have a similar view of the raven as the Tlingit. What follows is a Tlingit tale about the raven.

The Raven and the Seagull

When the Great Spirit created the world a long time ago, he built boxes out of the cedar trees that grew in the forest. And in these boxes he kept and stored all the items he created.

This was the time before humans, and the Great Spirit gave these boxes to the animals that lived in the world before humans. Inside the boxes were mountains, fire, water, wind, seeds, oceans, trees— everything the world needed to flourish.

And when the animals opened their boxes, these items were released out into the world. But something was missing. There was no sun, no moon and no stars in the world. None of the animals could see or find anything.

The animals looked to see who had the box that contained light. It was the seagull. But the seagull was greedy. He refused to open the box, holding it tightly under his wing.

All the animals pleaded with the seagull to open the box so the world would have light and they could see the world that the Great Spirit had made. But the seagull refused.

The raven, because he was smart and could sometimes trick people into doing things they didn't want to do, tried to persuade the seagull.

The seagull knew the raven would try to talk him into opening his box so he held onto it tighter.

But the raven did not utter a word. He picked up a thorn and stuck it into the seagull's foot. The seagull yelled in pain but didn't open the box. Finally, the raven pushed in the thorn deeper until the pain caused the seagull to drop the box. Then out of the box came the sun, moon and stars that brought light to the world, and the first day began.

In the Haida culture is a story of how the raven created the world but quickly became bored with it. He created some creatures—men—who were trapped in a clam. The raven released them into the world but quickly became bored with them too. Then he found some other creatures—women—and the raven introduced them to the men. The raven was never bored again.

Another Pacific Coast creation myth has the raven flying away from the bird world because he is bored. When he left the bird world, the raven was carrying a stone in his beak but soon he got tired of carrying the stone and dropped it. And that stone was the beginning of the world.

Of course, there are several other stories where the raven just acts silly and gets in trouble, like the following tale from the Nuu-chah-nulth people of Vancouver Island.

Raven Annoys Octopus

One morning, as the tide went out, the old people came to sit and watch the ocean. As they sat there, they saw a woman walking along the beach. Her hair was long and strung into eight braids. Her name was Octopus, and she had a digging stick in her hand. She was going to look for clams. She sat down on a rock at the edge of the water and began to dig.

Soon, another person came along the beach. That person was tall with glossy black hair.

"Look," one of the old people said. "Here comes Raven. He is going to bother Octopus."

Raven walked down to the rock where Octopus sat and stood beside her.

"Octopus," Raven said in a loud voice. "What are you doing?"

Octopus just continued to dig with her stick. Raven stepped closer.

"Are you digging for clams?" Raven asked again in a louder voice.

Octopus kept digging.

Now Raven moved closer to Octopus. "Are you digging for clams?!" he shouted.

Suddenly, Octopus stood up. She dropped her digging stick. Her eight braids turned into eight long arms. Four of the arms grabbed Raven and four held onto the rock.

"Yes, Raven," she said, "I am digging for clams."

Raven struggled to get free. The tide had turned and the water was rising. "Thank you for answering my question. Now let me go."

But Octopus only held him tighter. "Raven," she said, "it is clams that I am digging for."

The water was rising deeper around them. Again Raven begged her to let him go, but Octopus held him tight. The water came over their heads.

"Octopus can hold her breath longer than Raven," one of the old people said as they watched. After a long time, Raven drowned.

"Don't worry about him," the old people said. "He will come back to life again. His cousin, Crow, will help."

The next day, just as the old people had said, Raven came back to life. However, it was a long time before he bothered Octopus again.

Finding the Raven

The raven is a special spirit animal. Similar to the coyote, the raven is not only a creator of the world but is also a trickster and a cultural hero. The raven continually saves the world but also causes trouble because of his trickster playfulness. In a sense, the raven is a contradictory animal, much like humans.

The color of the raven is also a contradiction. The raven appears to have black feathers, but if you view the bird's feathers close up, you'll notice they have a blue green iridescence. And in many Native cultures, the color black is not viewed negatively; it represents the mystery of life and the search for truth.

The raven is seen as a shape-shifter animal that not only travels between the earth of humans and the spirit world but is also comfortable in both realms. The raven is extremely curious, a gatherer of secrets and knowledgeable about secrets. In short, the raven seeks the truth.

The raven is a clan animal especially for Native people living along the Pacific Coast of Canada as well as for the tribes on the east coast of North America.

The raven is a symbol in the Native American zodiac for those born between September 22 and October 22. If you were born under the sign of the raven, are part of a raven clan or follow the raven as a spirit guide, you are a searcher for truth and a messenger for your people. You have strong spiritual power, and people can feel it when they are near you. They may not know what they are feeling, but they know it's coming from you.

The raven has intelligence and the ability to respond quickly and is decisive when the need arises. The bird is known to be quite charming, adaptable and can shape shift, or transform itself, to suit the environment it lives in. The raven is energetic, likes shiny objects and is known to communicate well, especially with other animals. But at the same time, ravens seek solitude and spirituality.

If you encounter a raven, something magical may happen to you. Pay attention to your dreams in case they give clues for the near future. You may notice coincidences a few days after the dream. These coincidences may or may not hold meaning for you, but do not try too hard to figure them out. Just be aware of their presence.

The appearance of a raven may be a sign of change. That change may be positive—that you are about to shape shift into something different, someone more spiritually aware and confident. But you must be prepared to let go of your old self to allow the new one to appear.

Change can also have negative connotations such as impending danger. But the raven isn't the danger; the bird's appearance is a just sign for you to keep a lookout. Some Native cultures see the raven as a sign of good fortune, and its appearance as a warning of danger could be the influences of when Europeans arrived in North America.

Of course, because a raven is a playful trickster, the appearance of the bird could mean nothing.

You should call on the raven if you have had a difficult and traumatic childhood or other life-altering experience. The raven animal spirit can help you rediscover the playfulness, freedom and the joy of innocence in your life. It can help you see the magic in your life, especially if the world seems gray and dull to you, and you seem to be in a rut.

Since the raven provided many gifts to humans, the animal is also a symbol of healing. You can call on the raven if you are need of physical or emotional healing, and everything you've tried hasn't worked. The raven is especially helpful when someone you love requires healing but that person lives far away from you. This bird's ability to fly long distances allows it to send a healing message or prayers and thoughts to your loved one.

The simplest way to call the raven into your life is to go outside and listen for the calls of the bird. Once you find the raven, pay attention to its calls and become familiar with them. The raven has many calls so it may take a bit of time to distinguish between the sounds.

Spending time in the dark is another way to call the raven spirit to you, but don't see the darkness as a bad place. See it as a place of mystery—a place to spend time alone, meditating and breathing slowly in order to help discover the mysteries of life.

Organizing a healing circle may also help you or someone you wish to help, especially if that person lives a fair distance from you. Invite friends and family to your home in order to send thoughts and prayers to the person who needs healing.

The raven is a complicated spirit animal, a creator and a trickster creature, and despite what Europeans thought and felt about the bird, it is a powerful spirit guide that should be welcomed with open arms.

EARTH

Bear

THIS CHAPTER DISCUSSES brown, black and grizzly bears in the temperate regions of North America. The polar bear animal spirit is discussed in another section of this book.

Bears are large and powerful animals, and thus, the animal spirit associated with them is one of strength. Many Native groups in North America feature a bear in their mythology because the animal is seen as a major being, both physically and spiritually. And almost every community within 500 miles of the Canada/U.S. border (and farther north) lived near bears. People respected the animals and told stories about them.

The bear, because it is at the top of the food chain and has no predators save for humans, is known as a protector in the animal kingdom where it makes its habitat. That's why the bear in many Native cultures is a symbol of leadership and is considered wise. Bears are not only great hunters, able to fell a moose or easily grab salmon from a rushing river, but they also are omnivorous, which means they eat all types of food, including insects, honey and berries. The bear is called a grandfather and given the respect of an honored elder.

The people of the Haida Gwaii in the Canadian Pacific Northwest call a bear an Elder Kinsmen. When a Haida killed a bear, eagle down was sprinkled on the bear's body to show respect before the animal's meat and the hide was brought back to the village.

In some tribes, it was disrespectful, even dangerous, to insult bears. You had to avoid stepping on bear scat and could not mention the animal's name outside of certain ceremonies.

There is an Inuit story about a young hunter traveling on the land for the first time with an elder. Because the young man was excited to be on his first hunting trip, he wondered out loud if they would see a bear.

The elder shook his head at the young hunter. "You must not wish to see a bear while traveling on the land," said the elder. "In fact, you should not even speak out loud about bears while traveling on the land because the bears will hear you and come."

The young hunter nodded to respect his elder, but he didn't believe the story.

The next day, while the young man was out by himself looking for game, a large grizzly bear appeared before him. Fearful, the young hunter backed away from the bear. But then he heard a noise from behind him. He turned, hoping to see the elder who would help him kill the bear—or at least help him scare it away. But instead of the elder, there was another, even larger grizzly bear that had been following the young hunter's trail.

The young hunter had nowhere to escape. Even if he managed to kill one of the bears or scare it away, the other one would attack him.

Fortunately, the elder showed up just in time, and together the two men scared the two bears away. The elder and the young hunter left the area and quickly returned home so that the bears wouldn't follow them.

And from that time forward, whenever the young hunter went traveling the land again, he never wished that he would see a bear and never spoke aloud because he knew that if he did, the bears would hear and come to him.

Hunting of Bears

A few Native groups had taboos against hunting bears and eating bear meat. According to a study published in the *Journal of Ecology and Society* (2009), however, this taboo was probably quite localized. For example, the Southern Tutchone people of the Yukon maintain informal rules about grizzly bears that hunted salmon in the rivers near this village. In order to prevent immature and dangerous bears from fishing in the areas near the village, the people wouldn't bother the older bears that fished there. In some cases, they even encouraged the older bears to return. Grizzlies have a clear hierarchy, and the older and larger bears won't let younger bears into their hunting grounds. And because immature bears tend to get into more conflicts with humans, having older bears around helped make the village somewhat safer.

Many peoples did hunt bears but followed certain rules while hunting or followed strict rituals after killing a bear. According to the Algonquin people of eastern Canada and the United States, when a hunter killed a bear, he treated the animal's spirit with respect and uttered words one would use for a deceased family member. The dead bear was then draped in ceremonial clothing and hung from a pole along with offerings of tobacco. After the animal was butchered, the carcass was placed on a scaffold above the ground to prevent scavengers from eating the meat. The Algonquin performed these rituals because they and many other peoples believed that bears were related to humans.

Most groups also had rules against killing a mother or her cubs until the cubs were larger and could take care of themselves.

As noted earlier, bears are often called grand-fathers, but in other Native societies they are also known as the brothers to humans. This belief is reflected in many of the stories about bears, includ-ing the following story from the Cherokee.

The Cherokee Legend of the Bear

A long time ago, there was a boy who spent all his time in the woods. His parents scolded him for his idle behavior, but that didn't deter the boy. At the first light, he would leave his home and stay in the woods until it was dark. Soon, the boy's fam-ily began to notice that his body was covered with brown hair. His parents became worried about their son's strange appearance and also because the boy never ate at home.

"Don't worry," said the boy to his parents. "I find plenty to eat in the woods, and it's much better than the corn and beans we eat in the village."

But his parents insisted he stay home.

"It's too late," said the boy. "You can see that I'm already changing, so I can no longer live in the village."

The parents were sad because they loved their son and wanted him to stay with them.

"Come live with me in the woods," said the boy. "There is plenty to eat, and you won't have to work hard to get it. Living in the village is hard work and even so, we sometimes don't have enough to eat. However, if you decide to come and live with me, you must fast for seven days before you join me."

The parents talked it over between themselves and also with the members of their clan. Many people in the clan agreed that life in the village could be hard, filled with long days with not much food at the end. So the parents and other members of the clan decided to fast for the seven days. On the eighth day, they were going to head to the woods to live with the boy.

However, the leaders of the other clans tried to persuade the group to stay in the village. But they noticed that the people had already begun to change. They had spent seven days without food and were now covered in brown hair and were more interested in food they could get from the forest.

The other clanspeople were afraid, but the transformed humans told them not to be scared. "We are going to where there is always plenty to eat, and from now on, we will call ourselves Yonva. And when you become hungry and there is not enough to eat, come into the woods and sing to us. We will come to you, and our flesh will be yours to eat. Do not be afraid to kill us because we shall live always."

So the Yonva (bears) taught the other clan members their songs, and to this day, bear hunters still sing the same songs when they are hungry and in need of meat.

In other stories, bears play a wide variety of roles. Sometimes the bear is an evil spirit that eats humans or administers justice to those who have done wrong. The bear could also be a bumbler who is fooled by trickster characters, or it has a tendency to get into trouble. It can also be noble and a morally upright character.

The Cree, the Lenape, the Abenaki, the Penobscot, the Iroquois, the Seneca and the Shawnee, among others, have stories in which the bear character is a giant human-eating monster. In Cree, this creature is called Katshituashku, which means the Stiff-legged Bear. The Lenape, the Shawnee and the Mohicans call the bear Yakwawaik, which, depending on the dialect, can mean the Naked Bear, the Hairless Bear or the Big Rumped Bear.

Other societies have names that are a variation of either stiff-legged or naked bear.

At first, it was believed that these descriptions of a large, stiff-legged and hairless creature was the result of Native peoples finding the fossilized remains of mastodons and creating ghost stories to describe these "hairless creatures." It was also believed that these stories could be the cultural memory of early peoples who hunted mammoths and mastodons. However, these theories are much disputed.

In these stories about bears, the naked bears are depicted as huge, violent animals that kill humans and must be hunted down and killed or defeated either by guile or in battle. In a sense, they are not really bears but monsters that resemble bears.

Bears are also seen as animals that can heal and guide humans. Because bears can still fight when severely injured, they are seen as animals capable of healing their own wounds. So bears are closely associated with medicine and healing. Healers and shamans are known to carry a bear claw in their medicine pouch to increase their healing abilities.

The Cherokee have tales about bears and their knowledge of healing bodies of water. In these stories, when a bear is wounded, either in a battle with another animal or by Cherokee hunters, the animal takes a long journey to a mysterious mountain lake.

Upon arrival at this lake, the bear plunges in and swims across. Once the bear reaches the other side, it is completely healed.

In the final story in this chapter, a tale from the Mik'maq people of New England and the Maritime provinces, the bear spirit Muin finds medicine to heal the people.

How Muin Became Keeper of the Medicine

In the beginning of time, the people lived in harmony with the land, their brothers and sisters and the plants and animals. The people knew all their brothers and sisters were there to help them live, so they sang songs to celebrate. One spring day, Muin, the bear, was in the forest, and he heard the songs. The people were singing a song to Muin so he moved closer to them to see what they were doing. They made offerings to Muin and asked him to help them find the medicines that would help them thrive.

Muin realized he would have to make a journey to the spirit world in order to find the medicine the people requested. During the spring and the summer, Muin ate all that he could because he knew his journey would be a long one. In late fall, he looked for a lodge so his body would be safe while he was on his journey. And just before winter arrived, he went into the lodge and fell into a deep sleep.

While his body slept, his spirit traveled into the spirit world, where he collected many of the medicines the people had asked for. Muin asked the council of the plant people for some of their medicines. The plant people agreed but told Muin that he first must promise to cultivate and fertilize the land for them so they could come back every year. Muin accepted the offer and asked the other animals to do the same. The plant people shared their medicines with him.

Finally, Muin realized his journey was over, and it was time to return to his body. But before he did, he visited one of the human women in a dream and told her of his return. He asked her to arrange a feast for him, and in return for her kindness, she would be forever known as Miumiskw, the Bear Woman.

The woman agreed. To prepare for this feast, Muin told Miumiskw which berries she should pick and the order in which they should be picked during the year. He told her which fish should be caught and how they should be caught. He told her which animals they should hunt and how they should be hunted and used.

With the help of her people, Miumiskw prepared a feast the way Muin had requested. And a few days later, Muin joined the people for the feast.

A sacred pipe was lit and shared among the people to honor his return.

And to this day, Muin tills and fertilizes by digging for food and berries, and the plants continue to grow. In the winter, he returns to his lodge so he can journey to the spirit world. And the people celebrate his journey with a feast in the spring and fall, using the foods and medicines that Muin had shared with them.

Finding the Bear

Bears are strong medicine. If you see the bear as your spirit animal, then you see yourself as confident with a commanding personal presence. When a bear like you walks in a room, people pay attention. You're protective of your family, almost to the point of aggressiveness. Being a bear means that creativity and insights come to you during the winter months or during times of solitude.

While bears can be noble leaders, they should watch for overconfidence. Sometimes bears may see smaller animals as weaker and not as important. But as many stories show, the bear, although he thinks he is strong and powerful, may come across as bumbling and silly. Bears are confident but they shouldn't use that confidence to overpower others; they should listen to others.

Bears are known for their fierce tempers, and when blinded by anger, they can lash out and hurt those closest to them, even when they don't intend to.

If you come across a bear while hiking in the woods, or if a bear appears in your dreams or during meditation, it is a sign to pay attention to. Bears can represent wisdom, healing, protection and insight. And meeting a bear, either physically or in dreams or during a spirit quest, tells you that you are near a sacred place, and that your presence has been noted and is being studied.

That said, you should never go on any quest, physically or otherwise, searching for bears because these animals are temperamental. Their territory must be respected, and if a bear comes to you, you should respect it.

If you wish to call on the bear spirit animal, it's best to spend time alone at home, or in a private space without any visual or auditory stimulation such as the TV, the computer or music. You might wish to sit alone in the darkness to get the feeling of being in a cave. Consider this activity as "hibernating" like a bear and connect with any insights that might come to you during this time.

In order to experience the physical sensation of being a bear, stand tall with your head held high. Adjust this posture throughout the day and you may get a sense of the physical power of the bear. Speak clearly, using your diaphragm to add authority, but not volume, to your voice.

Bringing out the bear spirit animal is one way of helping you deal with a difficult situation, such as an unhealthy relationship where you need to set a physical or emotional boundary with another person. The bear can also help you find the confidence to start a difficult project or to stand up for yourself when needed. As a healing spirit, the bear can assist in coping with health issues.

Because bears are considered to be grandfathers and brothers to humans, they should be honored, respected and never taken for granted.

Buffalo

THE TRUE NAME IN NORTH America for the buffalo is American bison, though people still refer to these animals as buffalo. In this book, "buffalo" will be used. For thousands of centuries, millions of buffalo roamed the Great Plains of North America, over 50 million prior to the arrival of the Europeans. The herds were so large that it took several days for the buffalo to pass a single point.

It is no wonder that buffalo are a key spirit animal to Native peoples, especially for those cultures that lived on the Great Plains, such as the Creek, the Sioux, the Blackfoot, the Odage, the Caddo, the Cheyenne, the Cherokee and the Cree as well as many other peoples.

The average male buffalo stands over six feet tall, weighs between 1000 and 2000 pounds and has a body length between 10 and 12 feet. Female buffalo are smaller, standing under six feet tall, weighing between 790 and 1200 pounds with a body length between 7 and 10 feet.

The key feature of the buffalo is its large head and massive hump over its shoulders. Both sexes have horns, and the head, shoulders and forelegs are covered in long, dark fur. Buffalo can live for about 25 years in the wild.

Because buffalo were so prevalent, they were one of the most important food sources for Native people who lived in and around the Great Plains. As well as using buffalo a food source, the hide was used to make a variety of items, including clothing and material to build tents and tepees. The fur of the buffalo was used for bedding and clothing. The sinew (longs bits of skin and muscles) was used as thread to sew items together. The bones and horns were used as tools, weapons and to denote status as well as for ornamental displays such as jewelry. The animal fat and dried dung were used to build fires, and buffalo hooves could be boiled down to create a type of glue.

It is no myth that Native peoples used every part of the animal, wasting nothing. Because of the buffalo's many uses, the animal was well respected and is engrained in Native folklore. Some of the stories describe how buffalo became one of the major sources of food. This Cheyenne story is one of them.

How the Buffalo Hunt Began

In the early days, the buffalo hunted humans. The magpie and the hawk were on the side of the people, for neither hunted the other. The two birds flew away from a council where it was decided that a race would be held between the animals and humans in which the winners would be allowed to eat the losers.

The race course covered a long distance around a vast mountain. One of the swiftest animals to enter the race was a buffalo named Neika, or Swift Head. The people were afraid and doubtful of how they would do in the race because of the great distance. The magpie and the hawk offered to race for the humans.

All the birds and other animals painted themselves for the race, and since that time, they have been brightly colored. The water turtle put red paint around his eyes, and the dark-colored magpie painted his belly and shoulders white. At last, all the animals were ready for the race and stood in a row at the start line.

Once the race started, the animals ran and ran, making loud noises instead of singing to motivate them to run faster. All the small birds, turtles, rabbits, coyotes, wolves, flies, ants, insects and snakes were soon left far behind. When they approached the mountain, Neika was in the lead, followed by the magpie, hawk and then the people; the rest of the animals were strung out along the way. The dust from the animals' scampering feet rose so quickly that the racers could not see what lay ahead.

As they were flying along the course, the magpie and the hawk could see animals and birds all over the ground; they had run themselves to death, and the earth and rocks turned red from their blood. All around the mountain, Neika led the race, but the magpie and hawk knew they could win and kept up with Neika until they neared the finish line. Then both birds swooped by the buffalo and won the race for the people.

Because the two birds had won the race for the people, the buffalo told their young to hide from the people who were now going to hunt them. The buffalo also told them to take some human flesh for the last time, which the buffalo still had from a previous hunt with the people. The young buffalo did as they were told and stuck the piece of human flesh in front of their chests, beneath their throats. The people do not eat that part of the buffalo, saying it is part human flesh.

From that day forward, the Cheyennes began to hunt buffalo. Since the magpie and the hawk had been on the people's side, the people do not eat these birds but the use their beautiful feathers as ornaments or wear them on their clothing.

Although hunting buffalo was a regular part of life for many of the peoples on the Great Plains, capturing the animal was not easy. Despite their large size, buffalo are able to run at speeds of 40 miles per hour over short distances. So hunting the animal was dangerous; it was not uncommon for people to be killed or injured during a hunt. Prior to the late 1500s, Native people did not have horses, so they found ingenious ways to hunt buffalo, especially if the herd was large.

At one site in northeast Wyoming (called the Ruby site), archeological evidence shows that Native hunters chased a herd of buffalo into a corral they had built. And once the buffalo were herded into the corral, they were trapped and therefore easier to kill.

But the most spectacular way that Natives hunted buffalo long ago was through the use of a buffalo jump. Using this method, a group of people, often an entire village, chased a herd of buffalo over several miles. The animals soon formed a stampede, at which time they were guided toward a high cliff, known as a buffalo jump. The buffalo would then fall over the cliff to their deaths. Any animals not killed by the fall were quickly dispatched by the hunters waiting at the bottom of the cliff.

This method of hunting buffalo not only provided the people with large quantities of meat and other supplies, but it also gave them a surplus, which they traded to other groups for various items.

A number of groups, like the Blackfoot, had a sacred stone, an Iniskim, that they used in ceremonies to call the buffalo back from their migration. These stones were usually fossilized shells or something similar that they found on the ground.

Some of the stones were shaped like animals, which is why they were considered sacred enough to be named after the buffalo. The following story tells of the discovery of the first sacred buffalo stone by the Blackfoot people.

The First Buffalo Stone

Long ago, before there were horses, there were buffalo, but they soon disappeared. The people hunted deer, elk and other game but these animals became depleted as well. There was no game for the people to hunt, and they began to starve.

One day, a very old woman was collecting firewood when she heard someone singing. She followed the sound and found a small rock. "Take me. I am of great power," sang the rock over and over again.

The woman picked up the rock, and it taught her a special song to sing. She took the rock back to her husband and told him what had happened. "Get the men together and we will teach them this song to sing to bring the buffalo back."

The men gathered in a lodge, and the old woman formed a square on the floor using some buffalo chips and sage. Once everyone was seated on the ground, the stone began to sing. "The buffalo will drift back...the buffalo will drift back," sang the rock.

Then the woman told the younger men, "Go to the top of the buffalo jump and arrange many buffalo chips in a line. Then wave a buffalo line (a rope made out of buffalo sinew) over the chips four times while singing like you did in the lodge."

The young warriors did what she said. They also sang. So did the people in the lodge. And the fourth time that the young men waved the buffalo line, the buffalo chips turned into real buffalo and ran over the cliff.

Since that time, the people honor the sacred stone and use it to call the buffalo back.

Humans were not the only dwellers on the Great Plains that depended on the buffalo. Buffalo were the natural prey of wolves, cougars and other predators. Scavengers relied on buffalo carcasses as their major food source. Birds used the molted fur of dead buffalo as a building material for their nests. The constant grazing and movement of the buffalo kept the grasses of the Great Plains short, allowing many animals, insects and plants to thrive. These same creatures and plants would not have survived if the grasses were allowed to grow taller.

The dominant influence of the buffalo on the Great Plains and in other parts of North America made the animal a keystone species. Its presence was vital to the existence of the entire Great Plains ecosystem.

Unfortunately, when the Europeans arrived in North America, the eradication of the buffalo began in earnest. The animals were slaughtered by the millions and used only for their hides; the rest of the carcasses were left behind to rot. The building of the railroad across the continent also infringed on the buffalo's territory, making it more difficult for the animals to survive. By 1887, a census put the buffalo population at 541.

The destruction of the buffalo also led to much hardship for the Native peoples who relied on them for survival. In fact, the U.S. government introduced a policy to remove the buffalo as a means to undermine the way of life of Native peoples.

Over the years, efforts were taken to protect the buffalo, and some groups began to establish captive herds to help replenish the population. By 1995, the buffalo population was about 150,000, with most of the animals living on privately owned ranches.

Many Native groups had rituals, dances and prayers that referred to the difficulty of hunting buffalo. Buffalo are given a special place of honor and respect in several myths—their spirits bring sacred knowledge to humans. The animals are considered by some to be so spiritually powerful that their horns and hides are often used for regalia and religious artifacts. Even in other regions where the buffalo is not as sacred, the animal is considered a positive influence, associated with endurance, strength and protection.

Tribes with buffalo clans include the Caddo, the Osage and the Pueblo tribes of New Mexico.

Finding the Buffalo

If you are associated with a buffalo clan or follow the buffalo as a spirit animal, then you have everything you need, and deep down in your heart, you know you are provided for.

You are considered quite generous with others and always try to see the good in people. If you are a person with a buffalo spirit animal, you are confident and relaxed in achieving your goals. Despite this, your behavior can be unpredictable at times, especially when harassed.

If you encounter a buffalo in the real world, in a dream or on a spiritual journey, it may mean it is time to clear out the clutter, thoughts and emotions you don't really need. It may also be a sign for you to stop feeling sorry for yourself and realize that you have many strengths, qualities and resources within you to call upon.

One of the most sacred animals is the white buffalo, and if you encounter this animal, it is considered strong medicine. The appearance of a white buffalo could mean the future arrival of a miracle or some other momentous event. You are also about to enter a period of peace, and your spirituality will increase exponentially.

Call on this spirit animal if you are feeling the pinch of poverty, whether because of lack of money or support or because your body and spirit is drained of energy. The buffalo can guide you if you're going through a period of tremendous struggle. When you're about to begin a major project and you need assistance to see it to the end, the buffalo animal spirit can be called upon to help.

Calling on the buffalo isn't difficult. One way to call on the buffalo is to hold a ceremony in which you give your personal items away. Gather friends and family together, asking each person to give something that is of value to them. That special item is then given to someone in the group. Then for the next seven days, in your prayers, thoughts or meditation, give thanks for what has been provided to you, rather than asking for things.

It also helps to stand upright, hold your hands out with your palms pointing upward as a gesture of openness. Then form fists for a minute. When you open your hands, breathe deeply and imagine that the force of the world is entering you through your lungs and your hands. This is a posture of acceptance.

The buffalo was not only a creature that offered physical comfort and food to Native peoples, but it also aided in spiritual healing and cultivated inner strength with an instinctive trust in life.

Cougar

THE LARGEST CAT IN NORTH America and one of the deadliest predators, the cougar is a feared yet respected animal in many Native cultures. Cougars are also called pumas or mountain lions, but the cougar is closely related to the lynx, the bobcat or even the domestic cat than it is to any other feline.

Cougars are masters of the hunt. They can easily bring down a deer or other large prey, and they also hunt so quietly that the prey is unaware of the attack. It was the cougar's stealth in hunting that many Native peoples both honored and feared.

Cougars are carnivores and true predators because their diet consists only of the animals they hunt. So hunting is integral to a cougar's survival and plays a major role in its existence. Unlike the wolf, that hunts mostly in a pack and usually takes the lame, the old or the young, the cougar hunts alone, not really caring if the animal it is tracking is weak or strong, old or young.

The cougar's ability to take down a large healthy animal without making the slightest sound resonated with the Native societies that lived near the cougar's habitat. The cougar's skill at patiently and silently tracking its prey until the time was just right for the pounce and the kill was the model that many Native groups used to teach young warriors how to hunt.

Cougars are long and lean animals, seemingly made completely of muscle. The average male cougar weighs between 150 and 265 pounds and is between 38 and 77 inches in length. Female cougars are much smaller, weighing between 80 and 132 pounds, but they are skilled hunters, especially when taking care of their cubs. Mother cougars will take on much larger animals, such as a bear, in order to protect their young.

A mother cougar hunts the equivalent of one deer every four days to feed her young until they are ready to hunt on their own. A lone adult cougar only needs to kill the equivalent of one deer every two weeks. Cougars also feed on smaller animals such as rabbits, mice and goats.

Because cougars are lone hunters, they usually have to cover a larger area, sometimes over 400 square miles.

Prior to 1492, cougars ranged throughout most of North America. They also live in Central America and parts of northern South America. But in the last 500 years, they were exterminated in the eastern area of the continent so they are found mostly in the West. Much of the folklore and stories about cougars comes from the Native cultures in those areas.

The cougar was considered an elder brother that could not only teach people about hunting but also had mystical qualities and could move silently both in the light and in the dark. However, to some tribes, the cougar's stealth had more sinister meanings.

Cougars are usually quiet, and to hear its scream or to see one was considered an omen of evil to a few Native tribes. And because cougars' eyes reflect light at night, this further added to the mystical and sometimes feared aspect of the animal.

Overall, the cougar had powerful medicine that it would share if those seeking that medicine treated the animal with proper respect and reverence.

Cougars appear in many Western culture stories, usually as a wise and powerful creature willing to help humans.

The Cougar, the Wolf, the Fox and the Bobcat

A long time ago, the Shoshone used to live in harmony in a forested area with many rivers. There was plenty of water and food, so life was good and the people were happy.

One day, a warrior group of vicious little people attacked the Shoshone. The warriors were experts with the bow and arrow and drove the Shoshone out of their lands.

The Shoshone held a council to decide what to do. They decided to send their medicine man on a journey to undertake a vision quest to figure out how to get rid of these little people. The old medicine man headed into the forest, following a bright star that led him into an opening in the trees.

In the middle of this clearing was the wolf, the fox, the bobcat and the cougar. The cougar had a head of a man, and his paws resembled human hands. The old medicine man was scared because he had never seen anything like this in his whole life.

"Do not be scared," said the cougar. "The other animals told me you were coming, and we are all spirits here to help you. What do you need?"

The medicine man told them about the vicious little people that had driven his people from their lands. He asked if the cougar and the other spirits could help get rid of them.

The cougar held a short council with the other spirit animals and then turned to the medicine man. "We will help, but on one condition," said the cougar. "If we get rid of these little people, the Shoshone must promise to never hunt the cougar, the fox, the wolf and the bobcat. You must stay away from us. And if you promise to do that, we will help you."

The cougar told the medicine man to return to his people. "Tell the people what I told you," he said, "And make them promise never to hunt us, and we will help."

So the medicine man followed the same star back to his home and his people. He told the people what the cougar had told him. But many warriors didn't believe him and still wanted to hunt the cougar, the bobcat, the fox and the wolf.

"What I say is true, and I will show you if you follow me to a great council with the cougar and the other animals," said the medicine man.

Because the people had chosen the medicine man to get answers, they agreed to follow him. Everyone, even the children and women, followed that bright star all the way back to the clearing in the woods.

In the middle of the clearing were the four animals, including the cougar with the head of a man and paws that were hands. The people were afraid when they saw the cougar.

"Do not be afraid," the cougar said. "We are here to help you get rid of the little people that drove you from your homes. But only if you promise never to hunt the cougar, the bobcat, the fox and the wolf."

Because the cougar was a powerful animal, the people agreed.

So the spirits started singing their prayers. And the old medicine man flew into the air. Lightning shot down from the sky, turning the forest into fire. It killed all the vicious little people, but the Shoshone were protected because they were in the clearing with the cougar and the other spirit animals.

When the fire went out, the medicine man was returned to the ground. "We have helped you," said the cougar, "so you must keep your promise."

And the Shoshone never again hunted the cougar, the bobcat, the wolf or the fox.

In the eastern part of North America, especially in areas around the Great Lakes, there is a mythological creature called the water panther—also called Mishibizhiw, or Gichi-anami'e-bizhiw, depending on the Native culture.

These underwater panthers were monsters that opposed the Thunderbirds, the great spirits of the sky. The water panthers lived deep in the lakes and rivers and could create storms and cause havoc on those who lived near the water or traveled on it.

These water creatures usually had the head and body of a cougar or sometimes a lynx. They also had scales along their backs, the horns of a buffalo or deer and other animal body parts, depending on the story. Underwater panthers had long tails that were often made out of copper, which was a precious metal in the mid-1840s, about the time this story originated.

It was taboo to take copper from certain parts of the lake or from specific islands, especially Michipicoten Island, the third largest island in Lake Superior. This island was said to be the actual home of Mishibizhiw. To take copper from this island was to steal from the underwater panther itself and bring on its wrath.

During the 1840s, there was a copper rush around this part of Lake Superior, and Europeans were mining copper from islands that the Natives considered taboo to mine. Several boats and ships were sunk by storms during this time, and the local

Natives blamed these deaths and storms on the anger of Mishibizhiw.

The Natives who lived along the Great Lakes sang or said prayers to honor or placate Mishibizhiw before they ventured out on the water. Since Mishibizhiw and the Thunderbirds were seen to be in eternal conflict, these songs and prayers were also meant to restore balance between the two entities, at least for a temporary period while the people were out on the water.

The following story from the Wisconsin Chippewa is about two young women who encounter the water panther.

The Underwater Panther

There was once a big lake, and Native people lived all around it. In the middle of the lake was an island of mud, which made it impossible to paddle straight across the lake. If people in one village wanted to go to the village on the opposite side of the lake, they had to paddle all around the edge of the lake to avoid the island of mud. They stayed away from the island of mud because it was said a terrible monster lived near it.

One day, one of the villages held a dance, and the people from the other side of the lake left in their canoes to go to the dance. Two women who were going to the dance started their journey late, after everyone else from their village had gone. The women were sisters-in-law, and one of them was rather foolish. She was steering the canoe and headed straight across the lake to the island of mud. The other sister warned her not to go that way, but but it didn't do any good.

The first woman carried a little cedar paddle with her but did not use it for paddling. She carried it everywhere with her. As they got to the middle of the lake, they started to travel near the island of mud, and as they did so they saw a hole of clear water. The water was swirling around like a whirlpool, and as they started to cross that bit of open water, a panther came out and twitched his tail across the boat and tried to turn it over.

The woman picked up her cedar paddle and hit the panther's tail with it. As she was hitting it, she said, "Thunder is striking you!" The paddle cut off the panther's tail, and the end of the tail dropped into the boat. It was a solid piece of copper about two inches thick.

The panther ran away through the mud, and the two women laughed hard.

One of the women said, "I guess I scared him. He won't bother us again." The two young women continued their journey to the other side of the lake, and when they reached land, one of the women gave the piece of copper to her father.

Many of the people believed the copper tail of the underwater panther had magical powers. Everyone wanted a little piece of the tail to carry for luck in hunting and fishing, so the people gave the woman's father a blanket in exchange for a tiny piece of the copper. Her family became rich from selling pieces of the tail of the underwater panther.

Finding the Cougar

The Creek, the Caddo, the Chippewa, the Shawnee and some other Native groups in the southwestern parts of the United States have cougar clans. As noted, cougars are seen as powerful medicine because of their hunting skills, but there is also something sinister behind the animal.

Because cougars can move silently both in the day and the night, they are seen as spirit animals that can move easily between the physical and spiritual worlds. People who are of the cougar clan or who follow the cougar as a spirit animal are adept at exploring the mystical side of life—a hunter of visions and dreams. That said, these skills should not be used to lash out and harm others, as cougars are apt to do, but to provide meaning and guidance to others.

People who have the cougar as their spirit animal move quietly and stealthily through life, seemingly unnoticed, but they always have a goal in mind.

And when the goal is in sight or it is the proper time to act, cougars will strike quickly without hesitating in order to achieve their goal, usually surprising others.

And while cougars are graceful with wonderful balance, there is a wildness about them. They prefer to spend time alone rather than socialize but also enjoy being with family.

If you encounter a cougar in any way, consider it a rare and wonderful event, but be wary and respectful. Don't approach the cougar too quickly, just observe the animal and move on. Seeing a cougar in real life or in your dreams indicates that now is the time to make a decision—do not procrastinate, and do what needs to be done. Try to be clear and open to others about what you want, but move slowly without anybody noticing until it is time to react, or you may lose what you are seeking.

If you need balance and grace in your life, it is a good time to call on the cougar. Also, if you are in a position of power and are indecisive about what to do or can't figure out how to move forward, calling on the cougar can be helpful. And the cougar spirit can guide you if you are overwhelmed and need to make decisions about your priorities.

One of the best ways to call on a cougar is to set aside some time to be alone, meditate quietly and listen for any sounds or notice any unusual scents come your way. Don't try to identify these sensations; just be aware of their existence.

Also, try to move with stealth—maybe take up hunting. If you don't wish to hunt, follow someone you do not know (albeit not threatening in anyway) for a short period without being seen. These actions may bring messages or visions from a cougar animal spirit. Accept that you have a wild side to your personality.

The cougar doesn't like to be seen, so any view or vision you may have of a cougar animal spirit will be extremely brief. And be aware that the animal spirit is strong medicine that must be respected.

Coyote

OF ALL THE SPIRIT ANIMALS, the coyote is probably the one animal most closely connected to Native spirituality. The coyote is a major figure in Native folklore as creator, hero, trickster, clown, antihero, and many times all of these characters combined.

In these stories, the coyote is characterized as having great intelligence and adaptability that he uses for good, but he also tricks and cons other animals and humans. This character also gets into trouble because of its trickster ways and serves as an example of how not to behave. But for the most part, the coyote gets out of trouble by using his intelligence and cunning.

Tricksters are neither good nor bad, neither stupid nor overly smart. In a sense, coyotes are similar to humans, who, depending on the situation, can be unpredictable. The animal's habitat was also widespread, including most of North America prior to the arrival of the Europeans. These could be the main reasons why the trickster character is so popular in Native cultures.

Another reason for the coyote's popularity in stories has to do with the Native concept regarding humor. In order to connect to the sacredness of the world, to reach the Creator or to gain perceptions about the world, be it material or spiritual, laughter is an important factor. This is almost the opposite of the European concept of taking a somber and serious approach in connecting with the divine.

Laughter allowed Native people to be free from preconceived ideas, to open up their minds and souls to all the world has to offer. In short, laughter relaxes the mind, body and spirit, and through that laughter you become free to connect to the sacredness of the world.

The trickster aspect of the coyote shows people that surprise and the unexpected play a major role in life. And also, although the Creator may have made humans in his own image, the reason why humans are flawed yet still wonderful is that the Creator is similar to them.

The trickster/cultural hero comes in several guises, the most popular being the raven (sometimes the crow) and the coyote. But the coyote plays a deeper role than that of the crow or raven.

In many Native cultures, especially the groups west of the Mississippi River, the coyote is the trickster. But unlike the raven in other trickster stories, the coyote can adopt other roles, including that of the Creator, who can also be the trickster.

The Nez Perce are a people who traditionally lived in the Pacific Northwest in the region that now includes Montana, Idaho, Washington and Oregon. In the following Nez Perce story, the coyote uses his trickster skills to create the world and the people.

Coyote and the Monster

A long, long time ago, no people lived on the earth. At one time, animals and other living beings roamed the earth, but a monster appeared on the land, eating everything in sight. Only the coyote survived because he was quick and cunning, and the monster could never catch him.

Coyote was angry at the monster for eating all of his friends and family. So Coyote climbed the tallest mountain in the range and tied himself with rope to the top of a tree to entice the monster.

And when the coyote saw the monster walk by in the valley, Coyote yelled at the monster.

"Come eat me, you silly monster!" Coyote said. "I am the last animal alive; see if you can eat me."

The monster was big but could not reach the top of the mountain. And every time he tried to climb, his weight pulled him down. He tried to blow Coyote off. And though the wind he created was stronger than the strongest blizzard, he could not blow Coyote off the mountain.

The monster realized that Coyote was extremely clever, so he thought of a new plan. Instead of being angry at Coyote, he invited him to his lodge.

Coyote agreed to go to the monster's lodge but only if he could visit all of his friends first.

"I ate all of your friends," said the monster with a friendly smile. "They are in my stomach."

"Can I visit them to see if you treating them right?" said Coyote. "That way I will know if you are a good creature, and I can visit you at your lodge."

That is an even better plan, thought the monster. *I will eat Coyote when he visits his friends.* So the monster opened his mouth wide, and Coyote slid down the monster's long throat and into his stomach.

Coyote's friends were sleeping because the monster had eaten them. But this was Coyote's plan in the first place—to trick the monster in order to get into his stomach without being eaten.

Using his teeth and claws, Coyote cut the monster's stomach open, killing the monster. All of the animals woke up and escaped. They thanked Coyote for saving them.

And now that the monster was dead, Coyote decided to break him apart so he wouldn't rise again to eat all of the animals. Coyote decided to create a new animal.

He broke the monster into many pieces and threw all the pieces into the four directions, north, south, east and west. And everywhere a piece of the monster landed, people were created.

As stated earlier, coyotes were popular as spirit animals to Native cultures because the animals were widespread. Their habitat today covers almost all of North America save for the High Arctic. However, there are coyotes in much of Alaska.

Coyotes are similar in appearance to wolves but are much smaller, with an average weight of 44 pounds, a body length of 30 to 39 inches and a shoulder height of 12 to 19 inches. The coyote's ears and muzzle are pointed and its fur is shaggy.

Coyotes are less social animals than wolves. They can live in family packs between three to seven animals, but for the most part, these packs only exist in habitats where coyotes regularly hunt larger prey. In areas where smaller prey are more readily and easily available, coyotes live primarily on their own.

Some coyotes have been tracked traveling hundreds of miles away from where they were born in order to mate, which helped expand the genetic diversity of the animals and prevented inbreeding.

Like wolves, coyotes are highly intelligent animals, but they are often better hunters than wolves. In fact, coyotes are considered one of the most successful carnivores in the world. Coyotes are also fast, one of the fastest animals in North America, able to reach a top speed of 40 miles per hour.

In some parts of the continent where coyotes and badgers co-exist, the two animals often work as a hunting team. The coyote uses its keen sense of smell to find burrowing animals under the soil, and then the badger uses it powerful front claws to dig out the prey. When it is captured, they share the catch equally.

The flexibility in a coyote's hunting style, its diet and social structure make it one of the most adaptable animals around. Even when the Europeans arrived and used intensive methods to eradicate animals like the coyote, coyotes continued to survive.

In fact, the elimination of the wolf helped the coyote spread its range even farther in North America. Coyotes increased their interbreeding with wolves and domestic dogs but that didn't dilute their gene pool. In many cases, the interbreeding with wolves in northern Canada has created larger coyotes with a better ability to live on the tundra.

Coyotes are quite adept at living in urban areas, and as cities became more numerous and larger, coyotes have quickly adapted to an urban lifestyle.

The intelligence, adaptability and hunting capabilities of coyotes were no doubt noticed by Native peoples during the 20,000 years that coyotes coexisted with humans in North America. In almost every story in Native cultures, although the coyote is a trickster, even a bit of villain, it is never seen as stupid, and in many cases, is cast as a noble creature.

In the following Blackfoot tale, we see how the coyote helped to create humans.

The Old Man and Coyote

Long ago, when the earth was new, only the Old Man, known as Na-pe, lived in the world. Except for his friend and sometimes enemy, A-pe'si, the coyote, and a few buffalo, Na-pe lived alone. There were no other people or animals.

But Na-pe changed that. Maybe he shouldn't have, but he did. He changed the world because he was lonely.

On the day that Na-pe decided to change the world, he was sitting by his fire, bored and lazy. He had no reason to go hunting because he had a young buffalo to eat. His lodge was built and his fire was hot enough. He was comfortable, but he had nothing to do.

His friend A-pe'si was nowhere to be seen. But even if the coyote was with Na-pe, they wouldn't be talking because they'd had an argument and were on bad terms.

So Na-pe spent his days poking at the fire, throwing rocks into the river, walking around the land for a bit and smoking his pipe. "It would be nice to have someone to talk to," he said out loud. "Someone like me."

He walked some more, poked the fire some more, threw more rocks into the river and smoked his pipe. And then he realized something. "I am the Old Man. I can make anything I want," he said to himself. "Why shouldn't I make another one like me and have a friend?"

It was a wonderful idea, and Na-pe immediately started working on the project.

He went to a pond and carefully examined his reflection in the calm water so he would know what to make. Then he felt his body, counting all the bones so he could know his shape.

Then he took some clay, formed bones from the clay and baked them in the fire to harden. When the bones were firm, he removed them from the fire. Some of the bones were acceptable, but others were crooked or too thin or had broken during the baking. So Na-pe tossed those bones to the side.

He used the best bones and formed them into the shape of a man. He used sinew from the buffalo to tie the bones all together. Then he smoothed the bones with buffalo fat, padded them with clay mixed with buffalo blood and stretched buffalo hide over the whole creation.

Then he sat down, lit his pipe and spent much time looking at his creation. It wasn't exactly what he wanted, but Na-pe thought it was better than nothing.

He blew smoke into the eyes, nose and mouth, and the man came to life. He sat the new man by the fire and gave him a pipe to smoke.

"I'm going to make some more," said Na-pe.

The Old Man worked all day making more men. It took him a long time because some of the bones weren't good, and he had to make new ones. The bones he didn't like, he added to the pile he had made earlier.

Finally, he had several men, and they all sat around the fire, passing the pipe around. Na-pe sat with them and was satisfied.

They lived together in the camp. The men learned to hunt, and Na-pe had someone to smoke with so they were all happy.

But the heap of discarded bones was a nuisance. Every time someone went in and out of Na-pe's lodge, they tripped over them. When the wind blew through the bones at night, they made a terrible noise. The bones also blew around in the wind, making more noise. Na-pe thought about tossing the unused bones into the river, but he was lazy. He left the pile of bones where they were.

Then Na-pe's friend A-pe'si returned from wherever he had been. A-pe'si looked at the newly created men over and over again for a long time. He told Na-Pe that he didn't like them. A-pe'si also didn't like the pile of discarded bones.

"You should do something with those bones," A-pe'si said to Na-Pe. "Make them into men as well."

Although Na-pe was lazy and didn't want to do all the work, he was getting annoyed with the pile of bones too. "All right. I'll make more men out of them," he finally said.

"And I will help you," said the coyote. "Because I'm so clever, I will make something much better than these poor men of yours."

So A-pe'si and Na-pe gathered the bones and tied them together with sinew to form their shape. Na-pe mixed the clay and the buffalo blood and pulled the hide over them all. The Old Man intended to make men like the ones he had created before, but A-pe'si kept interfering and changing the original design.

When they were finished, the Old Man and the coyote had something that looked like a man but was different. Na-pe looked them over and over, not sure what he had made. But there was something about them that he liked. And the other men liked them too.

So Na-pe blew smoke into the eyes, nose and mouth of the new creature, and woman was made. Na-pe and A-pe'si made more women, and instead of sitting by the fire to smoke like the men did, the women talked to each other.

A-pe'si was proud because he liked creatures that talked. Na-pe wasn't sure he liked them because he preferred creatures that sat around the fire and smoked. Although the two creatures were different, they all seemed to like each other. And when they got together, they made their own creatures—small creatures that grew into new men and women.

And Na-pe liked that because he was lazy and preferred to sit by the fire and smoke. So he didn't have to create these creatures anymore. He eventually made other creatures too, but they weren't as difficult to make as the men and women.

Coyote was pleased as well because the men and women were amusing and fun to watch, and he liked to trick them.

In other Blackfoot stories, the coyote and the old man character are the same person with the ability to create and fool others. In this story from the Sahnish people of North Dakota, the coyote acts like a regular trickster but does this to help others, such as humans. He not only brought the buffalo but also introduced fire to the people and taught them how to grind flour, how to find healing herbs and other skills.

Coyote Brings the Buffalo

In the first days of the world, a powerful creature named Humpback owned all the buffalo. He kept them in a stone corral near the mountains, where

Humpback lived with his only son. He didn't share any of the buffalo meat with the people.

Coyote didn't like Humpback's selfishness and decided something had to be done to change that. "Humpback will not share his buffalo," Coyote said to the people. "Let us go over to his corral and hatch a plan to release them."

Coyote and the people headed to Humpback's camp and saw the tall stone walls of the buffalo corral. The walls were too high for the people to climb. And the only way into the corral was through the back door of Humpback's lodge.

After scouting around the lodge and finding no other way in, Coyote held a council meeting.

"Does anyone have an idea of how to get into Humpback's corral and release the buffalo?" he asked.

"There is no way in," said one man. "We cannot get in, and Humpback is too powerful a creature for us to fight."

Coyote thought for a moment and came up with a plan. "Did you notice that Humpback's son has no pet to play with? I will change myself into a killdeer with a broken wing. And when the boy goes to the spring to get water, he will find me and want to help me. He will take me to his home and make me his pet, and when I am in the lodge, I will fly out the back door and scream. The sound of the killdeer will scare the buffalo into a stampede, and they will break down the walls and escape."

The people thought Coyote had a great idea. And the next day when Humpback's son went to the spring to get water, he found a wounded killdeer on the ground.

As Coyote predicted, the boy picked up the bird and carried it home.

"Look at this poor bird I have found," the boy said to his father. "This is a very good bird!"

"It is good for nothing!" Humpback shouted, looking at the bird. "All the birds and animals and people are rascals and schemers."

Humpback wore a blue mask above his fierce nose, and his eyes glittered through the slits of the mask. His basket headdress was shaped like a cloud and was painted black with a zigzag streak of yellow to represent lightning. Buffalo horns protruded from each side of the headdress.

"It is a very good bird," the boy repeated.

"Take it back where you found it!" roared Humpback, and his frightened son did as he was told.

As soon as the boy released the killdeer, it flew back to the people and changed into Coyote.

"That plan didn't work, but it makes no difference," said Coyote. "I will try again tomorrow. Perhaps a small animal will be better than a bird."

The next morning when Humpback's son went to the spring, he found a small dog lapping at the water. The boy picked up the dog at once and hurried back into the house.

"Look at this dog I have found," he said with glee. "It will make a nice pet, don't you think?"

"A dog is good for nothing, you foolish boy," Humpback growled. "I'll just kill it with my club."

But the boy held tight to the dog and started to run away, crying.

"Very well. But let me test it first," Humpback said. "All animals in the world are schemers."

Humpback took a burning coal from the fire and brought it closer and closer to the dog's eyes until it gave three rapid barks. "Okay. It is a real dog," Humpback declared. "You may keep it in the buffalo corral, but not in the house."

This was exactly what Coyote had hoped for. When night came and Humpback and his son had fallen asleep, Coyote, disguised as the dog, opened the back door of the lodge. Then he quickly ran through the buffalo herd, barking as he went.

Since the buffalo had never heard a dog barking before, they were frightened and started to stampede. The buffalo ran through the back door, and although Humpback was awoken by the sounds of hooves, he couldn't stop the buffalo. The animals crashed through the walls of the corral and escaped.

Humpback's son didn't care about the buffalo; he was looking for his dog. "Did you see my dog?" he asked. "Where is my dog?"

Humpback sighed. "That was no dog," he said. "That was Coyote. He has tricked us into letting loose all our buffalo."

And so it was that the buffalo were released to scatter and roam over all the earth because of a trick by Coyote.

Finding the Coyote

Despite being such a major spirit animal for many Native peoples, there are only a few coyote clans. Some anthropologists have theorized that coyote was too significant a spirit animal to have a clan named after him.

The coyote has many attributes, but as stated earlier, the one that seems consistent throughout Native cultures was the coyote's role as trickster. Even when the coyote creates the world or provides great knowledge or goods to humans, he is still considered a trickster. Coyote never takes himself seriously, even if he has created the world. In fact, in some legends, that is the reason why he created the world: he was bored and needed something to amuse himself.

The coyote represents laughter, fun and keeping a sense of humor, no matter how difficult life's hardships may be. The coyote always tries to find the funny or amusing side of a situation. Those who follow the coyote as a spirit animal do the same. That doesn't mean they are always clowns, but they never think they are too important to take themselves seriously. And they always like to bring those who take themselves too seriously down a notch or two by using humor and playing tricks.

There is nothing better to coyote than showing self-important people how silly they really are. The coyote is not a buffoon but a smart, sly character that loves a good joke, even jokes at his own expense.

Another common aspect of the coyote is the animal's survival abilities. Coyotes are great hunters and are extremely resourceful. They can adapt quickly to any situation or problem, no matter how difficult. Nothing throws off a coyote.

The coyote is a talented teacher and leader that leads by example in such a way that others learn by watching or interacting with the animal. Coyotes never really lead from the front and usually aren't the official leaders. They live among the people and will often be the one everyone turns to for advice, leadership or knowledge.

There is also a paradox, sometimes even hypocrisy, in the life of a coyote. But the coyote doesn't care about this because he knows the world is full of paradox and hypocrisy, as are the people who live in it. The coyote is one of the few honest creatures that accepts and understands this component of life.

If you encounter a coyote, especially on a spiritual journey, you are being visited by a major spirit animal. What the coyote may tell you, either through his actions or words, may not make sense—the words may even contradict themselves—but there is strong medicine at work. The coyote is not the kind of creature to give easy answers—he might even try to trick you. But if you listen carefully and pay attention, and look deep within yourself, you should be able to discern the message. Of course, that insight may take a long time to arrive—days, months, even years—but once you understand the message, it will all make sense. Never dismiss the coyote even if you cannot understand him or it seems as though he is trying to trick you.

Calling on the coyote animal spirit can be a mixed bag because the coyote gets bored easily. Sometimes he wants to help, sometimes he doesn't and other times he doesn't really care. If you make a point of seriously searching out the coyote, chances are you won't find him, even in the real world. The coyote is out there, but he is intelligent and has learned that for the most part, people searching for coyote are trying to get something from him or want to kill him.

The best way to find the coyote is by not searching for him. Have an open mind, understand the complexities of the world, realize that everything isn't always black and white, good or bad, and that things just are the way they are, and that's the way life has always been.

You could take a walk in the twilight or dawn in the wilderness or even in the city because coyotes are prevalent in urban areas. You may not find the coyote, but he may be there anyway, watching you. If you are open and ready, the coyote may come. Or it may not.

But there is one way that may help you access the animal spirit of the coyote, and that is to enjoy life. Do not take yourself too seriously. You won't find or connect easily with the sacred through somberness. You must relax and have fun in order to be one with yourself and the world. Laughter is indeed the strongest medicine. And the coyote loves nothing better than laughter.

Deer

FOR MANY NATIVE PEOPLES, deer were a primary source of food because the meat could last a long time when prepared properly, especially during the harsh months of winter. Deer hide was used as clothing, footwear, material for dwellings and was a key ingredient in instruments, such as drums, which were used in sacred ceremonies. The antlers of a deer, mostly a male deer, were used to create tools or weapons. Deer, like the buffalo, the salmon or the orca sacrifice themselves in order to feed humans, and thus, deserved respect and honor. Many cultures performed deer dances and sang songs or did other rituals of thanks when a deer was killed during a hunt.

Some Native groups had taboos about killing the mother of a fawn because this would not only rob the next generation of deer but could also bring bad luck or harm to the person who killed the mother.

The people had other uses for deer other than its being a source of food. The diet of the deer was instrumental in showing them which berries and plants were not poisonous. And because of this, the deer was seen as a teacher, a guardian of humans and a guide for survival in the natural world.

In forested areas in the eastern part of North America, deer were often seen as a sign of fertility, or in the case of a buck, a sign of male prowess and sexual strength. In some cultures, it is said that if a woman comes upon a buck, she will soon meet a man who desires her sexually. If a woman comes upon a doe, she is at a fertile time in her life.

And if a man comes upon a doe, he will soon meet a woman who will flirt with him and attempt to seduce him. And if a man sees a buck, he could be entering a phase of sexual prowess. These sightings can be seen as positive or negative, depending on the recipient's personal circumstances.

Deer are another of the most adaptable creatures in North America, with many species living throughout most of the continent. For the most part, this chapter discusses two prominent species of deer: the mule deer (sometimes called the black-tailed deer) and the white-tailed deer. Although the two species are closely related, the mule deer is the larger of the two, and it seems to bounce over obstacles, using all four legs to spring up into the air.

Mule deer are mostly distributed throughout western North America, while white-tailed deer mostly live in eastern areas. Mule deer prefer more open areas, such as meadows or fields, where it is easier to spot predators. White-tailed deer live in forested areas or where there is more underbrush. They tend to hide or quickly bound away from predators. White-tailed deer can leap gracefully over obstacles rather than bounce. They also flick their white tails as a warning to other deer.

Both species feed on a wide range of plant material, such as berries, leaves, grasses, shrubs and twigs, depending on the season. The animals eat as much as they can during the warmer months when plants are plentiful in order to put on weight. This extra weight helps them survive during the winter when they have to dig under the snow for food or live on a diet of twigs and pine needles.

Like the buffalo, deer were more plentiful in North America prior to the arrival of the Europeans, numbering millions upon millions across the continent. But deer are not migratory animals and tend to live in the same areas, sometimes moving up in altitude depending on the cycle of the seasons.

Uncontrolled hunting and deforestation of land for the development of farms and urban areas seriously affected the population of these animals.

For a time, especially near the beginning of the 20th century, the deer population in North American was disastrously low. Their numbers have increased as a result of habitat management, hunting restrictions and other measures, and though plenty of deer populate wilderness areas so that, for the most part, they are not an endangered species, their population is nowhere near the levels before 1492.

In this story from the Lenape, it is promised that there will always be deer in the world.

Meesink and the Creator

Years and years ago, the Creator was working on building the world. He was almost finished creating humans. However, all the animals got together and thought that creating humans was a bad idea. They decided to contact Meesink, a powerful spirit, for help.

"Messink," said the animals. "Since you are so powerful, could you go see the Creator and ask him not to create humans?"

Messink thought the animals had a good point. He said he would visit the Creator and pass on the animals' request.

Messink went up to the Creator's lodge and knocked on the door.

"Come in," said the Creator.

Messink went in and sat down, watching as the Creator worked on the humans.

"Creator, know that we love you and your creation of the world. It is wonderful place," said Messink. "But these humans…the animals and I don't think creating humans is a good idea. They are going to hunt all the animals until none are left. They are going to dig in the earth. They are going to chop down all the trees. They are going to fill the rivers, lakes and oceans—the blood of the earth—with poison. They are going to make the air stink. Creator, we do not wish to question you, but please do not make humans."

The Creator listened intently and nodded. "I understand what you are saying, but I have a deeper knowledge than you of what I am doing," said the Creator. "But still, we will have a contest to decide which decision is correct. Can you see that mountain over there, Messink?"

Messink turned to look out the window, and near the Creator's lodge he saw a huge mountain. "Yes, I see the mountain," Messink said. "What about it?"

"Whoever is able to move the mountain the farthest will decide what will happen," said the Creator.

"If you win, I won't finish creating humans. But if I win, I will continue, and I will put the humans on the earth with everyone else."

Messink went up to the mountain and leaned his back into it. He pushed as hard as he could, using all the magic he had. But he couldn't move the mountain.

Just as the Creator was about to take his turn, Messink heard a sound. He quickly turned to see what it was, and as he did so, his face hit the mountain. He face was smashed in, and he had wrinkles now where the skin had been smooth. He realized that he had just heard a deer rushing by.

Messink also realized that he was wrong to question the Creator's wisdom. He knew that the humans would be fine as long as they had the deer. They would need deer for their food, their clothing, their tools. They would use every part of the deer. And Messink decided he would help them.

"Forgive me for questioning you, Creator. I see your wisdom now," said Messink. "I see that there must be deer for the humans. Please put me in charge of the woodlands where these deer will live. And I will make sure that humans will always have the deer."

And to this day, Messink has kept his promise. He has taken care of the deer. Many great animals have existed in this world, but most of us have never seen them because they have disappeared. But the deer are still here. The deer are still protected by the people.

There is another lesson to be learned from Messink's experience: sometimes we need to be hit on the head by a mountain to realize that we are going against what the Creator has meant for us to do.

Many Native peoples in North America respect and honor the deer, and there are two basic deer-type characters in their stories: Awi Usdi, or the Little Deer, and the Deer Woman.

In most of the Awi Usdi stories, the deer is helpful to humans, a teacher of sorts, showing the people how to use nature and be respectful of it at the same time, as in this Cherokee legend.

Awi Usdi

A long time ago, back when the world was young, all the creatures of the earth, from the humans to all the animals, could speak to one another. They lived in peace. Those who hunted took only what they needed. The humans were like that too, hunting animals only when they needed food to eat or skins for clothing and other materials.

One day, the humans invented the bow and arrow. And they discovered that they could kill more animals with these weapons. So they started killing more animals than they needed.

The animals were worried, thinking that if the humans kept killing animals at this pace, they would kill all the animals in the world. The animals held a council to figure out what to do.

"We should fight back," said one of the bears.

"But how?" asked another bear. "The humans will kill us if we get too close to them."

"We can make our own bows and arrows," said the chief of the bears. All the other bears thought that was a good idea and started to make bows and arrows. But when the bears tried to use the bow, their claws made it difficult for them to shoot the arrow.

"We'll just cut off our claws," said one bear.

But the chief of the bears didn't think that was a smart idea. "If we cut off our claws, we won't be able to climb trees. And we won't be able to hunt or dig for food. If we don't have claws, then we are not bears."

The other animals discussed how they could protect themselves or fight back against the humans. But none of them could think of a way to do this.

When the deer finally met, Awi Usdi, the chief of the deer, knew exactly what they should do. "We cannot stop the humans from hunting us because that is the way of nature," he said. "But if they keep hunting this way, without respect for the animals, we will all die, and there will be none left to hunt. And then the humans will starve.

"I will talk to the humans and tell them this. And I will tell them that whenever they need to kill a deer, they must perform a special ceremony in which they ask permission to kill a deer. And then they must show respect to the deer spirit and ask forgiveness for what they have done."

Awi Usdi also told the animals that if the humans did not follow his request, he would use his magic against them. "My magic will make them lame," he said. "And they will not be able to hunt or do anything else."

The chief of the deer then went to the hunters at night while they were sleeping. He whispered in their ears as they slept, telling the humans what to do when they wanted to hunt deer. He told them about the ceremonies they must perform and how to ask for forgiveness.

The next morning, the hunters thought they had dreamt this story and were unsure whether they had actually heard Awi Usdi. But some of the hunters did honor the dream, and they did what they were told; they hunted only when they needed food or hides. And these hunters also asked for permission before hunting and asked for forgiveness after they killed a deer.

Other hunters disregarded the dream and hunted whenever they wanted to. They didn't show any respect or honor. And Awi Usdi used his magic to lame these hunters.

Soon, all the hunters of the people began to treat the animals with respect when they hunted. They only hunted when they needed to, and even though the animals and humans cannot speak to one another anymore, the people show respect and honor those animals that they have killed in their hunts.

Deer Lady can be the opposite of Awi Usdi. For the most part, Deer Lady is a shape-shifting spirit that can take on the guise of a beautiful woman, an old woman or a deer. In some Native cultures, she looks similar to the centaur—she has the upper body of a young woman and the lower body of a deer. In other cases, she can have the whole body of a woman but will have hooves instead of feet.

In Plains cultures, Deer Lady is a spirit that helps women who are infertile. In other cultures, she is more of an evil spirit that punishes adulterous men or disobedient children. In the basic Deer Lady story, a beautiful woman appears to a warrior at a dance, either off to the side of a trail or hiding in the bushes. She is the most beautiful woman the warrior has ever seen. The Deer Lady entices the man away from the dance or invites him into the bushes for an intimate encounter. The man, usually proud and conceited, accepts the invitation. Once away from everyone else, the Deer Lady and man engage in romance, but before their union can be consummated, she kills him by stomping him to death, or she puts a love spell on him and then disappears. And because of the spell, the man can love no one but her and spends the rest of his days searching for her.

However, if the man looks downs and sees the hooves of the Deer Lady and recognizes who she is, she will run away. If she has previously harmed others, tobacco and chanting can be used to banish Deer Lady from the area.

Finding the Deer

The Cherokee, the Iroquois, the Menominee, the Chickasaw, the Huron, the Osage and the Shawnee, among others, all have deer clans.

The Native American zodiac has the deer as the sign for those born between May 21 and June 20.

The characterization of the deer in the zodiac is at odds with other explanations. In this zodiac, the deer is defined as someone who is a great conversationalist, quick witted and lively, a bit narcissistic and more concerned about appearance than other deeper issues. However, if you follow the deer as a spirit animal, you have a deep connection to nature and are full of grace, but with strength. A deer is a keen observer but doesn't attract attention to itself.

To some Native peoples, because the deer showed humans which plants and berries were safe to eat, it is seen as a great teacher and a guardian from nature.

If you encounter a deer, either in the material world or on a spiritual journey or vision quest, it usually means that you will meet a stranger in the near future. The stranger will find you attractive and wish to pursue you sexually. This can be a positive experience, but the encounter may be negative or threatening, depending on the person's marital status.

If a deer comes close to your fire, it wishes to deliver a message from the spirit world. Ask it to come to you when you are asleep and talk to you then. It may, like Awi Usdi, talk to you in a dream, teach you something or offer some sage advice. A deer spirit is also a sign that you should also pay more attention to your intuition because you are the best judge in determining how to handle any challenges you encounter.

In the wild, deer may seem weak because it is an animal that is hunted and preyed upon. But deer are adaptable and can adjust to major changes in the environment much easier than most of its predators. Deer are also alert and observant and can quickly blend in to their surroundings when needed. And while deer may appear to be delicate and vulnerable, like Bambi in the Disney movie, underneath that seemingly delicate nature is a lot of muscle that can explode into action in an instant.

Dog

ONE OF THE MOST IMPORTANT animals to Native people was not a wild animal that they hunted or had to protect themselves against. As common in most other parts of the world, dogs were loyal companions to Native people in North America. They aided in hunting, tracking and killing prey for humans. Dogs were also used as pack animals, especially for the Plains and Inuit cultures. In times of famine, dogs could also be a source of food, and for a few Native groups, their hides were more prized than other animals such as the wolf.

Dogs are called human's best friend, but they were also one of the best and most reliable helpers for the Inuit of the High Arctic. The Inuit relied on dogs a great deal—their dogs are one of the oldest breeds on the planet. These animals were key to their survival in the harsh environmental conditions.

Inuit dogs, also known under the official breed of Canadian Eskimo dog, were instrumental in helping the people travel in the Arctic. These dogs pulled sleds of supplies, families and hunters over vast distances in order to search for food or to change camps for the season. The dogs also helped hunters by chasing and catching a wide variety of game such as caribou, seals and even polar bears. Often, hunters only had to yell *nenook*, the Inuit word for "polar bear," and the dogs took off on the chase.

The Inuit did not view their dogs as members of the animal kingdom like the polar bear or even wolves; dogs were considered another tool for human use. Even so, there was a close bond between the dogs and their handlers. Inuit dogs are known as a tough breed, loyal, hardworking and intelligent.

Unfortunately for the breed and for the Inuit, use of these dogs as working partners has faded over the past few decades since the introduction of the snowmobile. In addition, Inuit dogs suffered great losses and their numbers dwindled because of the systematic killing of Inuit dogs from the 1950s to the 1970s by government authorities such as the RCMP. Some believe this culling was done in order to destroy a part of the Inuit culture and to force the people to abandon their nomadic lifestyle.

The Inuit have a number of stories about dogs in their culture, but one of the most interesting is the story about the role that dogs played in the creation of Europeans, other Native peoples, the dreaded sea goddess Sedna and all the animals of the sea.

The Legend of the Sea Goddess

One time, long ago, there was a great blizzard in the far north. A handsome young stranger showed up at a family's igloo and asked the father for lodging. The stranger wore a necklace with two large canine teeth. Thinking nothing of the necklace, the father showed kindness by allowing the stranger to stay the night. But the next day, the stranger was gone, and the father only saw animal tracks outside the igloo.

"We were tricked," said the father. "That was no human. It was must have been my lead dog disguised as a human."

Later, the eldest daughter became pregnant, and the father believed the disguised stranger was the culprit. Worried about what this union would create, he put his daughter in a boat and paddled her out to a small island, where he abandoned her without food or water.

However, the lead dog secretly swam out to the island and left pieces of meat, such as liver, so the young woman wouldn't starve. The woman survived and gave birth to six babies. Three of the babies were fully human, but the other three had big ears and long snouts as noses.

The woman used sealskins to make a kind of slipper, and she put the three strange-looking babies into it and pushed them out to sea. As she did, she shouted, "You will be good at making weapons!" And the three children were swept to the south. It is believed that these children were the ancestors of all white men as well as other Natives, and only in this way are they related to the Inuit.

The next night, the father came to the island and saw his daughter and the other three children. He took them on his umiak, an open boat larger than a kayak, but when they were heading back to their home, a severe storm arose.

The father wished to spare the children but realized that if he didn't lighten the load, they would all sink, so he threw his daughter overboard. She tried to cling to the boat with her fingers, but he cut them off, and her fingers fell into the sea and became seals. She tried again to climb onto the boat, but her father cut off her hands, and her hands floated down into the water and became walruses.

The woman tried one more time to get into the boat, but her father cut off her forearms, which turned into whales. After that, she sank to the bottom of the sea, but she did not die. The woman became Sedna, or Taluliyuk, the half woman, half fish that controlled the seas. Sometimes Sedna would become angry at the people and cause the sea to rise and break the ice, killing those who stood on it.

Every new hunting season, the livers of the first sea animals killed are tossed into the sea as a gesture of thanks to Sedna and to request that she release more animals so the Inuit may feed their families.

Experts on the evolution of dogs disagree with the origins and actual details of the domestication of dogs. However, they do agree, and genetics proves the theory, that all domesticated dogs are directly descended from the gray wolf. They also agree that interaction between humans and wolves played a significant role in the domestication and further evolution of wolves into dogs.

The current thinking is that the domestication of dogs occurred sometime between 15,000 and 8500 years ago, and it occurred independently in different locations. Two of these locales include parts of Europe and Siberia. And once domestication took place, dogs became ubiquitous companions to humans throughout the world.

Humans and dogs derived much benefit from living together. The dogs had a regular food supply and were safer because humans were taller than dogs and could see predators at a longer distance, at least during the day. And even though humans used dogs for a variety of purposes, even food at times, the dogs could breed more successfully than wild dogs. And their litters had a better chance of survival because of the care humans gave them.

Because of their highly developed sense of smell, dogs were also useful to humans because they could not only track prey but could also hunt down the prey, which meant that their handlers didn't have to risk their lives.

Dogs also played a part in sanitation in the camp because they ate the meat scraps that would have attracted other predators. Dogs also warned their handlers of these predators and protected them. Many scientists have noted that the domestication and use of dogs by humans was one of the most significant factors in the survival of early humans and a key reason humans became such a successful species.

So as people moved from Asia, through Beringia—the continent that rose up in the Bering Strait during the last ice age—and into North America, they came with their dogs. Some even speculate that the use of sled dogs played a major role in allowing people to cross the vast glaciers that blocked the way into North America.

Whatever the case or the history, dogs arrived in North America during the Beringia migration and their use spread with the various peoples as they separated to become the Native cultures of the continent.

The main reason dogs were the only domesticated animal in North America is that, unlike Europe, Asia and other parts of the world, North America did not have any domesticated animals. In the course of human history, only a few of all the animals species in the world have been domesticated, and the major ones include dogs, sheep, goats, pigs, cows, horses, donkeys, camels, chickens, llamas and alpacas, among others. However, none of these animals was native to North America.

And although buffalo, elk and deer are now kept in enclosed areas and raised for meat and other products, they are still considered undomesticated wild animals because they are highly dangerous or skittish when approached by humans.

But dogs, being the only animal that lived closely with humans in North America before 1492, were important to Native cultures. Almost every Native culture has a story on how dogs became integral to humans. The following story comes from the Plains Cree.

Where Dogs Came From

One time, long ago, there lived a hunter, his wife and their only child, a four-year-old boy. The winter that year was bitterly cold. Deep snow covered the ground, and hunting was difficult because there was little game.

One day the hunter found the tracks of a buffalo and followed them for a long time. But it was too cold, and the snow was too deep for him to go far. So he failed to track the animal.

When he returned home, he stood outside his tepee, scraping the snow from his moccasins. Inside, he could hear his wife talking to their crying son. The boy was crying because he was hungry.

"Don't cry, my son," said the mother. "Perhaps your father has killed a buffalo. That's why he is late in coming home."

Hearing those words, the hunter knew he could not go inside his tepee empty-handed. He had to find some game that he could bring back to his family so they wouldn't starve.

He walked back into the cold night, praying that he would find some game. It was a hard, long night, but just before dawn he came upon more buffalo tracks and followed them. But it was a tough slog, and the man wasn't sure if he would catch the buffalo. He thought of his hungry family and kept going, but then he started crying, thinking he would never catch up to the buffalo.

Suddenly a wolf ran up to the hunter. "Why are you weeping?" asked the wolf.

The man looked at the wolf and said, "I need to catch this buffalo. My wife and child are starving, and if I don't bring back food, they may die."

"Then I will help you," said the wolf. "Hide behind these bushes, and I will drive the buffalo toward you. But use my bow and arrows, not yours."

The wolf ran off, and the hunter looked at the bow the wolf had given him. It was much smaller than his own and not as well made. But he remembered the wolf's instructions, and when he heard the buffalo being driven toward him, he took up the small bow and shot six animals, one after another. When the seventh and last buffalo approached him, however, the hunter took up his own bow and arrow and shot at it. The animal escaped.

The wolf returned soon afterwards. "What luck did you have?" asked the wolf.

"I killed six buffalo with your bow and arrows," replied the man. "But for the last buffalo, I used my own bow, and the seventh buffalo escaped."

"I told you to use my bow and arrow," said the wolf. "However, we have enough meat for many people."

The hunter and the wolf butchered the animals. The wolf requested they set aside portions of two buffalo for his wolf family, and they did. The man carried as much meat as he could on his back to his starving wife and child. They were pleased to see him because they were worried when he had not returned that night. But the woman and her child were even more pleased when they saw how much meat he had brought.

That night, they ate until they were full. And when they were done, they dismantled their tepee and camp and moved to where the butchered carcasses lay so they would have more buffalo meat.

The wolf and his family lingered fearlessly around the camp, but the hunter and his family didn't worry. They knew the wolf had helped the man hunt the buffalo.

The mother fed the wolves buffalo meat, and the wolves soon became tame. They even allowed her to harness a travois on their backs. And from then on, the wolves remained with the family and became their dogs.

Because dogs were highly regarded by Native cultures, there are many stories about how to treat dogs or what happens to those who mistreat them, as in this tale from the Lenape.

The Stubborn Girl

Long ago, when the Lenape lived in the east, there was a girl who was extremely stubborn, and everyone in her village knew this.

One autumn evening, when all the villagers were gathered around the fire for warmth, a dog appeared. He was wet and shivering because of the cold. The stubborn girl saw the dog first. She went over to the dog and pushed it over.

"Tell us a story! Tell us a story!" she shouted at the dog. "You probably know many things so tell us a story."

"Leave that dog alone," said the girl's mother.

But the girl was so stubborn that she pretended not to hear her mother. She pushed the dog over again. "Tell us a story! Tell us a story!" she again shouted at the dog.

Finally, the dog sat down. "Yes, I will tell you a story," the dog said calmly. "In three days' time, you will be lying under red dirt."

The girl suddenly became afraid. Her mother told everyone in the village, including the chief, what the dog had said to her daughter.

The dog had spoken the truth, because three days later, the girl disappeared. She was nowhere to be found.

And now the old people say. "A person should never abuse or question dogs. When a person leaves this earth, before they go to where Kishelamàkâng, the Creator, lives, they must cross a huge bridge. And guarding this bridge are all the departed dogs. Those who live a good life are allowed to cross the bridge safely and walk the road beyond. Those who do not live a good life cannot cross the bridge. And anyone who has ever harmed a dog will never be allowed to cross the bridge over to the other side."

Finding the Dog

The Menominee and Ottawa cultures as well as the Plains cultures have the dog as the symbol for their warrior societies. The Crow, the Hidatsa and the Blackfoot have the Crazy Dog Warrior Society, and the Cheyenne have the highly respected Dog Soldiers. Many of these dog societies still exist, representing Native soldiers who served in modern wars.

Because dogs are considered faithful friends and helpers for humans, loyalty plays a major role in those who belong to the dog clan or follow the dog as a spirit animal. People associated with the dog animal spirit are intelligent and trustworthy and look for the same attributes in their friends and partners.

Dogs are known for working for humanity, and those who follow the dog enjoy work that benefits humanity in some way.

If you follow the dog as a spirit animal, you may feel a strong sense of protection and being watched over. Dogs are faithful guides in your exploration of the spirit world, and they are able to warn explorers of any dark threats.

If you encounter a dog in your exploration, dreams or meditations, it can mean you are lonely and in need of companionship. You may be losing your resolve in a task, project or relationship. The dog will help you regain the motivation you need to move forward. Dogs are signs that you are in need of protection. They are also a sign that you should donate some of your time and effort to help others and that you should show loyalty to the important people in your life.

The importance of dogs as companions seems to be universal to almost all human cultures not just Native peoples. Dogs truly are humanity's best friend.

Horse

ONE OF THE MOST COMMON images of Native American peoples is the visual scene of painted warriors astride beautiful horses. We've seen this image on canvas, in photographs and on film. The connection between Native peoples and the horse seems timeless, an infinite bond between man and nature.

In reality though, Native Americans and their love and connection with horses is a modern concept. Archeologists and anthropologists say that Native peoples have lived on this continent for almost 20,000 years. But horses were only introduced to North America by the Spaniards after their arrival in 1492.

Most Native Americans did not encounter horses until the mid-1500s, and for some cultures, it was much later. So when compared to their total time in North America, Native people have had little time with the horse.

Even so, many Native cultures, especially those who lived on the Great Plains, quickly adopted the horse as a mode of transportation, and in less than a generation, the animal became an integral part of their lifestyle.

As in many other cultures around the world, the horse became the spirit of the wind, a fast-moving creature that wasn't bound by the limits of how humans could travel. The horse symbolized freedom because it allowed people to travel farther and faster and to hunt more easily. And because of the increased range, trade and connection with other peoples increased. Various peoples could now communicate with others they had never before heard of or met. The horse became a messenger image, one that expanded the boundaries of life, be it material or spiritual. In an extremely short period of time, the horse became a sacred animal with powerful medicine.

But the arrival of the horse wasn't a complete surprise to some Native Americans. For centuries there were stories and prophecies about the coming of a large animal that would change the world and how the people lived. Some people referred to the animal as the "giant dog" or the "medicine elk."

This story, from an unspecified Plains culture, provides a theory of why the horse arrived late in the lives of Native Americans.

Wind Horse

There was a time long, long ago when an animal called Wind Horse was known as the fastest of all the ponies. He felt no fear because no one wanted to harm him. If one of the people was injured, Wind Horse cared for the person and let him or her ride on his back.

One day, Wind Horse was running and feeling free when he heard a cry coming from the edge of the forest. He ran toward the sound and found a boy whose leg was caught in a bear trap.

The boy could not move because of his injured leg, so Wind Horse let him get on his back. The boy was surprised that the horse helped him because he had no name and no family. The boy had lived his life all alone.

And when the boy rode Wind Horse, a new sensation filled his heart. It was the feeling of freedom, something that Wind Horse had always felt. The boy now understood what it felt like to have a family.

But Wind Horse knew that the boy would not heal from his leg injury. The horse was taking the boy to the hunting grounds, a place for those who no longer lived in the real world. Although Wind

Horse knew that taking this final journey was sometimes a sad event, it was for the best. At the hunting grounds, the boy would be made whole and would never feel fear, hate or need.

As they rode on, the boy noticed that the trail had changed. The first part of the journey had been in the world he knew, where he was injured and alone. Then as they traveled farther, the place looked similar to a place he remembered from before he was born. But he also saw things he did not recognize, and he became afraid. He clung to Wind Horse with fear.

Because the boy was holding onto to him tightly, Wind Horse began to sense the feelings the boy was experiencing. The boy began to talk to the horse about his dreams of running through the leaves of the forest and of having a family or a friend to love. And Wind Horse understood the boy's dreams because even though he loved his freedom and enjoyed helping others, he, too, wished he had someone to love.

Wind Horse developed love for the boy, and as they approached the hunting grounds, something changed in the horse. While he worried he would no longer be free to run where he pleased by himself, Wind Horse knew it was even better to be with someone he loved.

And when he saw the vastness of the hunting grounds, he knew there were still plenty of new and different places for him to run. And now he had someone who could share it with him.

The boy realized where they were when they reached their final destination, but he felt no fear, hunger, pain or need. His injured leg was healed. And though this was his last journey, he had a friend, Wind Horse, to share it with him.

They both crossed over into the hunting grounds. Wind Horse knew he would never return to the real world. People would forget that he and his kind ever existed. Before he crossed over with the boy, Wind Horse asked the Creator to someday send a reminder to the people of the friendship he had with the boy.

And a long time later, the horse was sent to the people. It had been so long that they had forgotten that these animals had existed. But once they climbed on the horse's back, they remembered. They remembered what the boy had felt when he rode Wind Horse for the first time—that the feeling of riding a horse was like being with one's family.

When the Spanish brought horses to North America, they used the animals to carry their soldiers in the war against the Mayans and Aztecs and farther north into what is now Texas, California, Arizona and other states. The also used horses as pack animals to carry goods in and out of the Americas.

As the Spanish expanded their range of influence in the Americas, they gave Native Americans their first look at the horse. Initially, the Natives were afraid of the horse, calling it a large dog. The dog was the only animal most Native cultures had domesticated and used as a small pack animal.

But seeing the usefulness of the horse intrigued many, so some Native Americans took to raiding the Spaniards' camps in order to steal their horses. The Spaniards also took many slaves. And one of the tasks the Spaniards taught their slaves was how to take care of their horses.

However, when the Spanish left North America, it was deemed too expensive and wasteful to take their horses back with them. Gold and other precious goods were considered more valuable than horses, so they set the horses free into the North American "wilderness."

Some Native peoples found these animals roaming free, and many who had experience with the Spanish knew how to handle the horses. Other Native groups came upon wild herds of unusual animals they had never seen before, and at first, they feared the horses. But they quickly realized that horses could be useful. First, they used the horses the same way they used dogs—as pack animals. Then they realized that horses were strong enough hold a man's weight.

It didn't take long, barely a generation, but as soon as a people was exposed to horses, they became experts on how to capture, break and ride them. For many Plains cultures, such as the Blackfoot, Sioux, Crow, Teton and others, the horse revolutionized their lives. Horses allowed these people greater mobility, and they came into contact with other cultures never before encountered.

This contact had both positive and negative effects. More contact increased trade, alliances and intermarriage. But more contact also meant expansion of control, and alliances made could be turned against others who weren't part of the alliance. Having horses meant that warriors could strike enemies much quicker and from a greater distance.

Hunting was also dramatically different on the horse. No longer did hunters have to travel great distances on foot in search of buffalo and other game. And no longer did they have to wait for the buffalo to come near them; they could go to the buffalo.

Hunting buffalo was much easier and safer from the top of a horse. The hunters could travel at the same speed as the buffalo. And if an injured buffalo turned and tried to attack the hunter, it was much easier to get away on a horse than on foot.

Horses quickly became valued and had to be treated well. To disrespect and mistreat a horse was a crime to many people of the Plains, as noted in this Blackfoot story.

The Traveler

Long ago, there was a man called the Traveler who was a rich chief. When he was a young warrior, he had bestowed on him several honors, he fought numerous battles and he was a successful hunter. He became wealthy because he traded with people who were less fortunate than him. But he did not offer them sympathy or give them a fair deal. Instead, he used their misfortune to get what he wanted. He also gambled against younger and less cunning warriors and increased his wealth.

Although the people admired the chief's bravery as a young man, they did not love him. While other chiefs shared with those who needed help, the Traveler traded harshly. He treated his wives and children so badly that they all left him and felt hatred against him in their hearts.

The Traveler didn't care because he had many high-quality horses that he loved. But he wanted more horses. If a young warrior returned from a raid with a fine horse, the Traveler always found some way to cheat the warrior out of his horse. If a poor family had a fine horse as their only possession, he found a way to unfairly trade for the horse or forced them to give him the animal.

When the people gathered around the fire to dance and take part in ceremonies, the Traveler didn't join them. He went to where he kept his horses and gloated.

One day, the Traveler went to look at his wonderful horses. But in the middle of the herd, he saw an old, white stallion; it was ugly with a matted coat and crooked legs.

The Traveler became angry. Although he loved his horses, he only loved the ones that were fine and in good condition. He captured the old stallion, broke its legs with a club and left it to die. He returned to his lodge, feeling good for removing the ugly horse from his herd.

Then he realized that even though that stallion was ugly, he might get something for the hide. He returned to the dead horse, intent on skinning it, but the horse was gone.

That night, as he slept, the Traveler had a dream in which the most beautiful horse he had ever seen, a stunning white stallion, appeared to him. The Traveler realized it was the same horse he had killed earlier that day.

"If you had been good to me, I would have brought you more fine horses," the stallion said. "But you were cruel to me, so I will not bring you any horses. I will also take all the horses you have."

The Traveler suddenly woke up and ran to his horses, but they were gone. He walked around all day looking for them, but he couldn't find a single horse. He wanted to search some more, but he was so exhausted that he went home and fell asleep.

Again, the magnificent white stallion appeared in his dream. "If you wish to find your horses, they are near a lake in the north. It will take you two days to get there."

The Traveler woke up and headed north. When he arrived at the lake, however, his horses were not there. That night, the stallion came to him again. "If you wish to find your horses, they are in the east, by some hills," the horse said. "It will be two days before you find them."

Two days later, the Traveler found the hills but no horses.

The stallion appeared in the Traveler's dreams every night, telling him where to find his horses. And each time, the Traveler went to the place that the stallion told him to go to, but he found no horses.

One day, the Traveler stole a horse from a local village. But when he awoke, the horse was gone, taken by the white stallion.

To this day, the Traveler still walks, looking for his horses. On quiet nights, sometimes you can hear the sound of horses' hooves, followed by the footsteps of an old man. And if you are unlucky, you will see the white stallion, followed by a herd of fine horses, being chased by the Traveler.

Finding the Horse

Even though the horse came late to Native Americans, a few cultures, such as the Shawnee, quickly established horse clans. If you follow the horse as a spirit animal, you have endurance and strength to undertake long journeys, whether these travels are physical or spiritual. Some cultures believe the arrival of the horse in North America meant that the people could travel farther, including journeys deeper into the spirit world. So following the horse enables that exploration.

The horse animal spirit shows you have a desire for freedom and can quickly move away from mundane issues. You love to explore and find new byways, even if those journeys take you to locations that are considered unexciting.

If you're feeling held back by the world or constricted in any way, calling on the spirit of the horse can help. The horse can boost your energy, especially if you feel the need to travel but feel tired or rundown. If you have a need to explore more deeply in the spiritual world but are unsure of how to begin the journey, calling upon the horse spirit may guide you.

To call on the spirit of the horse is as simple as being around horses. You don't have to ride a horse; just find a place where there are horses and spend time near them. Being close to these animals will help bring the horse spirit to you.

You can also go for a walk, with no destination in mind, to get the feeling of being a horse. Don't think as you walk, just be in the moment, accepting all that comes your way and feeling your feet carry you forward.

Although the horse is a relatively new spirit animal to Native Americans, the animal itself changed the lives and lifestyles of many people over a short period of time. So the horse has great medicine that can change your life.

Polar Bear

BECAUSE POLAR BEARS ARE animals of the High Arctic, above the Arctic Circle, most Native cultures in North America have no exposure to the animal. Only the Inuit, and in some cases, the Dene, are familiar with the polar bear. But it is the Inuit who share the same habitat with this bear, one of the largest land carnivores on the planet.

First, it must be noted that the Inuit are spread out across North America, from the west coast of Alaska, across the northern arctic lands of Canada, through to the northern lands of Quebec and Labrador all the way to Greenland. Like the Cree, who are similarly spread out across North America, Inuit groups have similarities and differences.

One of the key differences between the various Inuit cultures is language. While there is an overall common language, or prestige dialect, each group of Inuit people has their own dialect, though they share similarities.

And one of the similarities all Inuit have no matter where they live or what language they speak is their respect for the polar bear. Much of Inuit spirituality, rituals, beliefs and taboos are deeply tied to their environment in the High Arctic. No single creature ruled the land because the harsh world they lived in could kill every creature with ease. To ignore these rituals, beliefs and taboos was, in a sense, to defy the environment they lived in.

The Inuit believed that all animals had a soul, called an *aniring*, the same way that people had souls. And these souls were part of the overall world, the *sila*. And that while all peoples and animals were unique and shaped by the body they inhabited, they were in a sense only borrowing the physical form from the *sila*, and the *aniring* persisted after death. When an animal was killed for survival purposes, the people had to complete rituals to placate the *aniring* of the animal so that it wouldn't take revenge on the person who killed it.

There is also a belief that creatures such as sea mammals, bears and plants were classified in different groups, and each could be ruled by a master of these animals, known as a *tuurngait*. A *tuurngait* could be evil and control other animals in ways to harm the local community. For example, a *tuurngait* for the sea mammals could force these animals to stay away from the community and cause the people to starve. Or the *tuurngait* for land animals could make a polar bear attack the community. There were specific rituals that people did to keep away, banish or placate various *tuurngait* that might cause harm.

The *tuurngait* of the polar bear was called Nanuk, or more commonly, Nanook. Some people believed that polar bears were actually men who lived in a different community. Those men lived as men while in their igloos, but before they headed outside, they donned the skin of a polar bear. When they stepped outside the igloo, they transformed into the bear.

The Inuit of Labrador believed that the polar bear was the embodiment of the great spirit because of its reputation as one of the largest land carnivores on Earth. And because there is little vegetation in the High Arctic for them to eat, polar bears are true carnivores. They are also one of the few true apex predators (a predator with no predator of their own) in their environment. Men hunt polar bears, but these bears are also one of the few animals that do not shy away from humans. To a polar bear, humans are no different than a seal or a walrus or any other creature in the Arctic: they are a source of food if necessary. The Inuit highly respect polar bears, and they keep their distance when they encounter a polar bear.

Male polar bears can weigh up to 1750 pounds and have a maximum body length of just over eight feet. Females are smaller at a maximum weight of 660 pounds and a body length of 6.6 feet.

Polar bears are a prime example of how quickly animals can evolve to adapt to a completely different environment. Around 100,000 years ago, polar bears and brown bears were the same animal. But even though they can still interbreed, the two are now different species. Polar bears have fully adapted to a difficult environment in which the average winter temperature is −40°F, and all of the land and much of the sea in winter is covered with snow and ice.

Because of the polar bear's size, it loses minimal body heat in its harsh habitat, and it can tackle larger prey with ease. The fur of the polar bear plays a major role in the animal's survival. The white fur allows it to blend in completely in the arctic environment, which helps in hunting, and the long and hollow hair follicles trap warm air, making the coat light in weight. It has recently been discovered that the skin under the fur of a polar bear is actually dark, which also helps keep the animal warm.

The bear's hollow hair follicles also assist with buoyancy when the animal is swimming. And polar bears are great swimmers, as comfortable in the water as they are on land. Their feet are slightly webbed, and their fur is slightly greasy. They can swim for hours at a time, sometimes up to 40 miles in a single swim. They can float without effort for a long time; in fact, even dead polar bears don't sink. Polar bears also grab onto drifting ice floes to help them travel for long distances.

And once out of the water, the polar bear's water-repellant fur allows it to remove all water in a single shake, ensuring that no ice forms on its coat.

The bear's breeding practices also show how the polar bear has completely evolved to its environment. Because of the vastness of the land, and the randomness in which polar bears hunt, they do not encounter one another on a regular basis. Therefore, there is no official breeding season for these animals. Interestingly, although polar bears can mate at anytime, cubs are always born in mid-winter because a female can delay the growth of fertilized embryos until she has built up enough strength and weight to survive the pregnancy.

The Inuit learned to hunt seals by watching polar bears hunt. Seals spend much time underwater in the Arctic, but since they are mammals, they must come up for air. But much of the surface water is covered by snow and ice, so seals make breathing holes in the ice. Every time they need air, they pop up to a breathing hole.

Polar bears can wait at these breathing holes for a long time. And once a seal shows itself, they scoop it out of the water. In the traditional Inuit way of hunting seals, the hunter finds a breathing hole and patiently waits for a seal to pop its head up, at which time the hunter strikes it with a spear.

It is said that the spirit of the polar bear, Nanook, showed humans how to hunt for seals. Nanook allowed humans to watch a polar bear hunting seals and other sea mammals. And because of this knowledge, humans were able to survive in the Arctic.

The polar bear is featured in many Inuit stories. The following story is one of the most popular.

Why the Stars Are in the Sky

To the Inuit, stars are living beings, sent to roam the sky forever. One of the stars is known as Nanuk, the spirit of the bear.

Nanuk escaped into the sky because one day he was being chased by a pack of six Inuit hunting dogs. Nanuk knew that fighting these dogs would be difficult, so he tried to run away from them. He ran and ran a long way over the ice, trying to escape the dogs. But they still pursued him. Nanuk ran for hours and hours, and still the dogs followed him.

In the excitement of the hunt, Nanuk and the dogs did not realize how close to the edge of the world they were getting. And once they reached the edge, they kept on going, jumping directly into the sky and becoming stars. To this day, Nanuk is forever pursued in the sky by that same pack of dogs.

The constellation that makes up Nanuk and the hunting dogs is one of the most prominent constellations in the winter sky, almost directly overhead by the middle of the winter night, but lying partly in the southern part of the sky. The Europeans called the constellation Pleiades. Also known as the Seven Sisters for its seven brightest stars (Nanuk and the six dogs chasing him), the constellation is one of the first to appear in the winter.

Although the polar bear appears in many Inuit stories, not all of them have a message or explain the origin of things. Some stories are just stories, but others show the correct way to act in the High Arctic.

The Woman and the Polar Bear

Long ago, there was village on the shores of a huge ice ocean. The people who lived on that land were called the Inuit. They were hunters and fishermen, eating seals, fish and other creatures of the snow to stay alive. In this village lived an old woman who had no husband, no children and no one to hunt or fish for her. But the people of the village shared their food with the woman as was their custom.

The old woman was lonely and longed for a family. She walked along the shoreline each day, hoping that one of the spirits would send her a family. One day she found a tiny polar bear cub all alone on the beach. At first, the woman feared that the mother bear was nearby and did not approach the cub because mother polar bears were very protective of their young.

But she watched the small bear and saw that the mother was not around. "Someone must have killed her," the old woman said to herself. She realized that the bear was, like her, all alone without any family. She walked over to the cub and picked it up.

"You will be my son," she told the bear. She took the cub back to her igloo and shared all her food with him. She named him Kunik. The old woman was no longer lonely, and a close bond formed between the two. Even the children in the village began to love Kunik, and they all played together.

Like all children, Kunik grew bigger and bigger. The children taught him how to fish, and soon he was one of the best fishermen in the village. Every morning he would go out for fish, and every afternoon he returned to the village with fish for his mother and other people in the village who had shared their food with his mother before Kunik had arrived.

He became a successful hunter, bringing the fattest seals home to the village. The old woman was extremely proud of Kunik. "He is the best fisherman and hunter in the village," she boasted to anyone who would listen.

Soon the other hunters became envious of Kunik's hunting skills.

"He puts us all to shame," they said. "He must be stopped."

And even though Kunik shared his extra food with the villagers, the hunters saw it another way. "He's too big and too strong. He is a danger to our families, and we must kill him."

A young boy who was one of Kunik's friends overheard the men talking and ran to warn the old woman and Kunik about the hunters' plan.

The old woman hugged her son and said, "I will not let them kill you."

She went from igloo to igloo, begging each man not to kill her son. "He is my child," she said. "If you must kill something to prove you are a great hunter, kill me instead."

But the men all disagreed. "He is too big and dangerous," said one of the men. "He is fat, and when we kill him, there will be enough meat to hold a massive feast for the whole village."

When the woman heard that, she realized the men would not be dissuaded.

"He is a danger to our children," said the other hunters. "We cannot let him live."

The old woman knew the men were determined to kill her son. She rushed home.

"Your life is in danger, Kunik. You must run away. Run away, and do not return, my child," she said, weeping and holding him close. "But don't go so far that I cannot find you."

Both of them had broken hearts as Kunik ran away and left the village, never to return.

The old woman and the children of the village were sad for a long time after Kunik left. The neighbors shared food with her, but she stayed in her igloo for many months.

Then one day, she felt it was time to go for a walk along the shore of the ocean, as she had done in the past. As she was walking along the ocean, up behind her came a big polar bear. Some hunters saw the bear coming toward the woman. They thought it was going to attack her and kill her, and they tried to warn her.

The bear came up to the woman. The old woman turned around, and when she saw the bear, it rose on its back legs. Surely she is dead, said the hunters when they saw this.

But this was not an ordinary bear. This was Kunik. He put his great paws around his mother and hugged her. "I love you," said Kunik. And his mother hugged him back.

To show his love for his mother, Kunik gave her fish and meat to eat. Kunik never returned to the village, but he met his mother every so often to bring enough food for her to eat.

The people of the village, the Inuit, knew that the love between the old woman and the bear was strong. And with pride and respect, they told others the tale of the unbroken love between the old woman and her son.

Finding the Polar Bear

The Inuit people don't follow spirit animals per se. There are no polar bear clans or totems built to honor the polar bear. The Inuit believe that all animals, like humans, have a soul or spirit, and that soul lives on after the animal has died. So if you kill a polar bear, you must honor its spirit because if you don't, it could seek revenge on you and your family in some way.

That said, the Inuit have deep respect for the polar bear, as a source of food, clothing and other materials. The Inuit hunt seal the same way that polar bears do, so the bear is also respected as a teacher.

The polar bear signifies strength, physical confidence and the ability to adapt to almost any situation or environment. The polar bear animal spirit signifies pure knowledge of who one is and what you can do. You have faith in the world, your place in it and the power of the earth.

Having a polar bear spirit means you are assertive in your communications and actions. Pause and observe what is going on around you, and when the time is right to move, act with direction and without hesitation. Also, only complete the task at hand rather than focusing on unimportant matters.

If you come across a polar bear, be wary, especially if it's a physical encounter. Do not go out searching for a polar bear unless you know how to protect yourself or have safeguards in place.

Polar bears are strong animals, as well as beautiful, but they should never be taken for granted or thought of casually. Heed the polar bear; its animal spirit commands respect.

Spider

SPIDERS MAY BE SMALL, BUT they are still considered spirit animals with great medicine by many Native cultures. Although spiders are normally seen as positive medicine, they have different meanings to different cultures.

On the positive side, the spider represents skill and intelligence for the Blackfoot, and patience and endurance according to the Ojibwa. A few people believed that the spider created the world by weaving it from her web—positive spider medicine is often associated with females.

To many Plains people, such as the Sioux, Dakota, Lakota and others, the spider is a trickster character, sometimes named Iktomi. For the most part, Iktomi behaves in silly, inappropriate ways, which gets him in trouble. However, there are also Iktomi cautionary tales in which he creates terrible trouble and acts violently. The Gros Venture people of Montana have a similar spider trickster character named Nihaat who acts the same way as the Iktomi character. Iktomi, though, is a much more violent character than Nihaat.

Iktomi and *nihaat* are Sioux and Gros Venture words, respectively for "spider." However, in later translations of Gros Venture stories, *nihaat* is sometimes translated as the color white, or white man.

Despite the mixed medicine of spiders from different cultures, most Native cultures believed that killing a spider was bad luck.

But one reason why spiders are considered strong medicine, especially in these modern times, is because of the creation and spread of one of the most identifiable and widespread symbols of North American Aboriginal peoples: the dreamcatcher.

The popular concept and most common purpose of the dreamcatcher is to help people while they dream. For many cultures, dreams come to people from the spirit world, rather than developing from within the person's mind. The dreamcatcher is designed to filter dreams so that bad dreams and nightmares get confused and become trapped in the web of the dreamcatcher. Good dreams are able to find their way through the web and into the mind of the sleeping person.

There are other interpretation of the uses of dreamcatchers and their origins, but many of these oral traditions have been lost or suppressed since the arrival of the Europeans. Unfortunately, dream-catchers are one of the Native items that non-Native peoples have appropriated for whatever reason and have attached their own uses and meanings.

The following two stories are the most common origin stories, though they they should not be considered the only, or true, stories of the creation of dreamcatchers.

The Story of the Dreamcatcher

During the time of the ancestors, there was a time when children began having bad dreams. As the children talked to each other, the bad dreams spread. Soon, almost every child had bad dreams, and their parents became worried.

The parents talked to the shaman and asked if he could help. He said he would, but first he would have to visit the spirit world to find the answers that might help. When he went on his journey, the shaman met up with the four elements of the world: Air, Fire, Water and Earth. The elements had heard of the children's bad dreams and wished to help. Together, the elements and the shaman dreamed for a long time. And as they dreamed, the elements came up with some ideas.

It was decided that Air would carry the bad dreams away.

And Earth would hold the dreams in her hoop.

Water would filter the bad dreams from the good ones.

And then Fire would burn the bad dreams away.

These were all wonderful ideas. But the elements had no way to catch the dreams in order to carry them, hold them, filter them and then burn them.

But grandmother spider had heard the shaman and the elements talking.

"I can weave a special web that will trap the bad dreams and let the good dreams go down to the dreamer," she said.

And the grandmother spider did, creating the first dreamcatcher ever made. The shaman took the dreamcatcher back to the people, who hung it where their children slept. The dreamcatcher was placed where the rising sun would hit it. The sun then burned away the bad and unwanted dreams trapped in grandmother spider's web.

And the children never had bad dreams again.

Dreamcatcher Legend

One day long ago, Asibikaasi, the Ojibwa grandmother spider, was spinning a web near the sleeping space of a *nokomis*, a grandmother.

Every day, the *nokomis* woke up seeing the light from the rising sun captured in the beautiful web. And she spent many hours watching Asibikaasi build its web even bigger.

After four days, the web was finished. But then one of the *nokomis'* grandsons came into her lodge a day later and saw the spider web. He wanted to protect his grandmother so he picked up a rock, ready to destroy the web and kill Asibikaasi.

"Don't disturb Asibikaasi," the old lady whispered to the young boy. "And don't destroy the web."

"Why not, Nokomis?" the boy asked. "Why do you protect this spider?"

"Because Asibikaasi spent a long time building a beautiful home," replied the *nokomis*. "When the sun rises in the morning, I see the light captured by it and it is wonderful. And Asibikaasi protects me by catching and eating all the insects that would fly in here and bite me. You should never destroy a web."

The boy nodded and left his grandmother, vowing that he would never intentionally destroy a spider web or kill a spider.

Later that night, Asibikaasi came to the grandmother in her dreams. She thanked the old woman for saving her life and her web. "For many days you have watched me spin and weave my web," said Asibikaasi. "You have admired my work, and you have saved my life. In return, I will give you a gift."

Asibikaasi smiled her special spider smile and moved away, spinning as she went. Soon the moon glistened on a magical silvery web moving gently in the window. "See how I spin?" she said. "Watch and learn. Bad dreams will be caught in the web and be trapped. The good dreams will be able to fit through the small hole."

The next day, Asibikaasi left the grandmother's place, but left her web, the first dreamcatcher. Because of the dream, the grandmother knew how to make more, so she made one for her grandson and for all the other children. And she taught the people how to make dreamcatchers until everyone had one.

Dreamcatchers are so ubiquitous that many believe that almost every single Native culture has dreamcatchers or believes in their medicine. However, prior to 1960, only the Ojibwa had dreamcatchers. In fact, the Ojibwa word for dreamcatcher is *asabikeshiinh*, which is the inanimate term for "spider."

During the 1960s and '70s when some Native groups became more political and vocal in their stances, many peoples began to adopt the dreamcatcher as a simple yet powerful symbol of solidarity among all First Nations peoples.

But despite the confusion of the origin of dreamcatchers, almost all stories point to the spider and its web as the inspiration for the design.

Although some people still call them bugs, spiders are not insects. They are arachnids, and based on their population and diverse habitats throughout the world, they have the seventh highest species diversity of all animals. There are over 40,000 species of spiders, and only one species of spiders are predators. Spiders mostly eat insects, but larger spiders have been known to prey on small birds and lizards.

Spiders use different methods to capture prey—jumping, trapping, fishing, mimicking—but the most common method is through the use of webs.

Most spiders produce a form of silk, a sticky and durable substance that they weave into webs of varying sizes and designs depending on the species.

The web is usually strung among a number of objects, branches, twigs, trees, and so on, and insects are trapped when passing through this seemingly open space. How spiders deal with their prey after they are trapped is almost as varied as the number of species that exist.

Some spiders create small traps with their silk instead of building a web. And other spiders stretch a single line of silk between two objects and continually patrol this line checking for prey. A few spiders even build communal webs in order to increase their trapping area. One such web was measured at over 200 yards wide.

Spiders come in many sizes, with the smallest having a body length of 0.015 inches, and the largest 3.5 inches with a leg span of up to 10 inches.

Although no definitive proof exists, there is a strong possibility that the positive and negative aspects of spiders may have played a role in how Native peoples perceived them. In areas where spiders are more dangerous, with stronger venom, such as in the southern parts of the United States, there seems to be more negative traits accorded to spiders. However, almost all Native peoples respected the spider as a skilled hunter and a talented builder.

In Swampy Cree culture, it was the spider that lowered humans to the earth, although she did warn them about it first.

The Story of Ehep

Long ago, the people did not live on the earth; they lived up in the sky.

One day the humans noticed that something was below them. It was a vast land, lush and beautiful. And they wanted to live there.

But the people had no way of getting there. Ehep, a giant spider, saw that the humans were looking longingly at the earth below.

"Do you wish to go and live in that land?" Ehep asked.

"Yes, we would love to live in that beautiful land," the people said. "Can you help us?"

Ehep thought about it for a moment and then told the people: "Yes, I can help you, but you must do what I say.

"I will build a large nest or basket. Everyone must get in and once you do, I will lower you down to the earth using my line. But there is one thing you must not do: you cannot look down on that land as I lower you. It is a long trip, and no matter how hard it is, do not look down. Even at the end, when you are getting closer, do not look down until I set you on the ground."

The humans agreed, excited to be heading down to this new land.

They all got into the nest that Ehep made. "Remember. You must not look down," Ehep said before lowering the humans. "If you look down at anytime, you will not be happy. The land you will live in will still be beautiful, but you will suffer and have to work hard to survive."

The humans agreed not to look down. Ehep lowered them toward the ground. It was a long trip because the land was far away, and the humans were so excited but wanted to know how much longer the trip was going to take. They were impatient to see this new land. So they forgot or dismissed what Ehep said and looked down.

It was the most beautiful place they had even seen. Full of greenery, lakes and rivers and animals and fish. Life would be easy for them on this land. But when they looked down, Ehep's string broke and the humans fell hard to the ground.

They survived, but what Ehep said was true. The land was beautiful, but the people were not always happy; they had to work hard and suffered while trying to survive on the land.

Finding the Spider

As noted, the spider as a spirit animal has some conflicting medicines. Some people see spiders as bad luck, something to be avoided. Or even a trickster out to confuse and con humans. Other people see the spider as a positive creature, a wonderful builder and hunter with amazing patience and endurance.

There are few spider clans, and the spider is not included in the Native American zodiac.

If you follow the spider as a spirit animal, you have a lot of patience. You have the ability to wait for long periods of time for the proper moment. And when that moment arrives, you strike, almost instantly, to achieve your goal. You are also a great builder who can connect "webs" between distant places and people, including connections with the spirit world.

Because many positive spider spirits in Native cultures are female, there is a feminine aspect to the spider as a spirit animal. But as with other feminine aspects, this should not be seen as a weakness. Spiders may be small compared to other animals, but they are strong survivors that can live in a wide variety of environments.

Although the web that spiders create—which can be interpreted as a form of creativity such as writing or art—may seem delicate and invisible, the spider's silk is a strong substance that is flexible and highly durable.

If you encounter a spider, especially in the spirit world, dreams or meditation, it means that it could be time to bring out your deepest knowledge and wisdom and incorporate it into the real world.

A spider may also indicate that some kind of trap is ahead and you should watch out for it. Or perhaps you are stuck at an impasse, but you can free yourself by being open to all the possibilities around you. You should work at becoming a more lateral thinker, instead of a linear one. A lateral thinker is more apt to see more different ways around a problem while a linear thinker usually can only see forward.

A good time to call on a spider as a spirit animal is when you feel trapped and need to find a way out. The spider can help if you're feeling limited, held back or if your life is out of balance in some way. The web of the world is infinite, and you can find the right path if you stay open to new opportunities.

Although spiders are relatively small, unusual looking and produce venom, they are patient, adaptable and create some of the most delicate but strongest materials in the animal world. There is much strong medicine from spiders.

Wolf

THROUGHOUT HISTORY, THE wolf was and still is one of the most feared animals. Vilified for centuries, wolves were hunted to the brink of extinction in Europe. And when the Europeans came to North America after 1492, they did the same to the wolves there. So many wolves were shot or trapped that by 1940, not a single wolf could be found in the western United States.

Native people had different views about the wolf than Europeans. The wolf was not an animal to be feared; it was to be respected and honored, which almost every Native culture in North America did. Like the bear, the wolf is considered to be like family to many Native peoples; the wolf is called a brother or a cousin to humans. But wolves are sometimes seen as much closer to man than bears. Whereas bears are mostly solitary creatures, wolves are social animals. They live in packs, and most of them are related to each other in some way. They hunt together, working as a well-organized team to bring down their prey, in much the same way Native groups hunted together.

Before they were almost hunted to extinction in North America, wolves, the gray wolf specifically, ranged throughout the entire continent. They live in a wide variety of environments from tundra to forests, prairie to mountains. They are the largest wild dog in the world, with a maximum weight of 175 pounds and a height of more than 26 inches.

Although they are skilled hunters, wolves rarely attack animals that can defend themselves or that can get away quickly. Wolves normally attack weak, old, young or injured prey, which is one reason why wolf attacks on humans are rare. There are no fully documented cases of a healthy, unprovoked wolf attacking a human.

A large wolf needs to eat an average of 5.5 pounds of meat per day, but they can go without food for several days. As noted earlier, wolves are extremely social animals. Their packs can range from five or six wolves during lean periods to almost 25 when food is abundant. Wolves are also adaptable, allowing their packs to grow and decline based on the availability of prey in their territory. A single wolf pack has a territory of anywhere from 8 to 5200 square miles. Alpha males may lead a pack for years, but if the alpha dies or is injured, the rank in the pack changes, allowing new blood to lead the group. They mark their territory by scent, by scratching and with prolonged periods of howling. Wolves will strongly defend their territory by fighting competing packs, sometimes to the death.

Wolves are also intelligent animals. When Europeans were killing buffalo by the millions, wolves figured out how to follow the sound of gunshots. They would then wait until the hunters skinned the buffalo and then they would feed on the carcasses left behind. When wolves were hunted from airplanes in Montana in the 1960s and '70s, they avoided open areas whenever they heard the sound of an aircraft. Wolves learned how to avoid the traps set by humans to capture them, and they even figured out how to trigger the trap and steal the bait.

Wolves are the direct ancestors of the modern dog. Although there is no conclusive evidence proving how wolves became domesticated and evolved into the domestic dog, there are a few theories. One of these theories is that humans adopted and raised orphan wolf pups, and then these animals passed on their less wild behaviors to the following generations, eventually producing the domestic dog.

Another theory is that wolves were attracted to the garbage humans left behind, and this proximity made the animals less fearful and more social around humans. Over time, the animals that were more social toward humans passed on this behavior to subsequent generations until they became completely domesticated.

The current scientific consensus is that the domestication of wolves into dogs occurred in Siberia and then spread throughout the world. It is believed that the first inhabitants of North America brought their dogs with them when they crossed the Bering Strait over 15,000 years ago; however, wolves were living in North America at the time.

This historical connection between humans and wolves is one of the reasons that the wolf is a key spirit animal to many Native cultures. The fact that wolves traveled in close-knit family-based packs, hunted together and raised pups as group resonated deeply with Native people because they too lived in a similar manner.

The medicine of a wolf is closely associated with loyalty, strength, courage and, not surprisingly, success at hunting. Wolf clans are one of the most common of all Native clans. Tribes in eastern Canada from around the Great Lakes to the Great Plains and to the Arctic and along the Pacific coast all have wolf clans.

The Cree believed that the northern lights were divine wolves coming to visit the earth. The Blackfoot called the stars in the sky the "path of the wolves." Before a hunt, Cheyenne shamans rubbed the arrows on the pelt of a wolf to give the hunters power.

The Cherokee never killed a wolf because they believed the animals' siblings would take revenge on the person who killed it. The Hidatsa who lived near the western shores of the Missouri River rubbed the bellies of pregnant women with the wolf skin in order to ease labor.

The Pawnee people in Oklahoma felt so connected to the wolf that the hand sign for the word "wolf" was the same sign they used for the word "Pawnee." The Pawnee in Oklahoma communicated with other cultures that didn't speak their language through a common sign language that had some minor differences depending on the tribe. And many people neighboring the Pawnee called them the Wolf People.

To the Sahnish people of North Dakota (among others), the wolf was key to the creation of the earth and of man, as noted in the following creation story.

Wolf and Lucky Man

In the beginning, there was sky and water. In the sky lived Nesaru, the sky spirit, and Wolf and

Lucky Man. Below the sky was an ocean, where two small ducks swam, making small, yet eternal ripples.

Believing there could be more to the world than just the sky and the water, Wolf and Lucky Man asked the ducks to dive down and find mud. The ducks did as they were asked.

Wolf took half the mud and built a vast prairie for creatures like him—creatures who liked to hunt. Lucky Man built hills and valleys where the people could also live and hunt.

Lastly, Wolf and Lucky Man pushed up the mud to create the banks of a river to divide their territories. Today, you can still see that river, now known as the Missouri River.

And so the world was ready for life.

Wolf and Lucky Man knew that the smaller creatures would come first, and from them they would create the larger animals. So they went into the earth to find two spiders, who they knew were to be the first creatures to propagate.

But when Wolf and Lucky Man found the two spiders, they were shocked to see that the spiders had no idea how to create babies. The spiders were so dirty and ugly that they weren't interested in each other anyway.

So Wolf and Lucky Man cleaned up the two spiders and taught them the facts of life. And so the spiders gave birth to the first creatures of the earth, eight-legged creatures like themselves. Over time, more creatures were born—those with six legs, and then those with four legs, and finally, those with two legs, the Sahnish People and all the other humans.

The Shoshone people, who are spread out through a large part of central west North America, from Nevada to California, from Oregon to Idaho and Wyoming, believe the wolf is a noble animal that created the world. In many of the Shoshone's stories, the wolf is bothered by the trickster coyote, who seems resentful or jealous of the wolves' power.

To the Shoshone people, the wolf not only created the world, but he also gave the world something else.

How Death Came to the Shoshone

In the early days of the people, since the wolf had helped create the world, he had the power to bring the dead back to life. And for a long time, the wolf did that, giving life back to those who had died. Humans lived and died over and over again.

And the Shoshone loved and respected the wolf because of this gift.

But the coyote was jealous of the wolf's power, and he wanted to trick the wolf so that the Shoshone wouldn't love him so much.

One day, the coyote walked up to the wolf and said, "Wolf, do you see that there are a lot of people in this world? Too many people."

"Please leave me alone, Coyote," said the wolf. "I have had enough of your tricks."

"No, this is no trick. Look around. There are way too many people. Soon the world will be too full and won't be able to hold them all," said the coyote. "I don't think you should bring them back to life after they are dead."

But the coyote was trying to trick the wolf. Coyote thought that if Wolf did not bring people back to life when they died, the Shoshone would be angry at Wolf and begin to hate him.

Wolf looked about and saw that the coyote could be right. There were a lot of people in the world. And if there were more people and no one died, the world probably couldn't hold them all.

"Okay, I will try it and see what happens," said Wolf. "I promise that I will not bring back to life the next person who dies."

The coyote agreed with the plan believing that he had tricked Wolf.

But the next day, Coyote's son went on a hunt with his pack and was killed.

Coyote begged Wolf to bring his son back to life. But Wolf said he couldn't because he had promised Coyote he wouldn't do it.

And in this way, death came to the Shoshone people. But it wasn't seen as a sad event; it was a way to make sure the world did not have too many people.

Finding the Wolf

Because the wolf is one of the most respected and honored of all animals, it is a common clan animal in Native cultures. The Creek, Cherokee, Chippewa, Lenape, Shawnee, Huron, Iroquois, Caddo, Osage, Tlingit, Tsimshian and Kwakiutl all have wolf clans. The wolf is also a valued symbol for peoples of the Pacific Coast, and the animal's image has been captured on many of their totem poles. The Lenape and the Shawnee have a wolf dance as part of their traditions.

The wolf is a sign in the Native American zodiac for those born between February 19 and March 20. If you are born under the wolf sign, you are deeply emotional, passionate and fiercely independent. The wolf can also be gentle, compassionate and nurturing. However, if left alone without guidance or love, a wolf can become obsessive, impractical and vindictive.

Because many Native cultures believed the wolf taught humans how to live, hunt and raise families within a community, the animal spirit is considered a wise teacher. And those who are born under the wolf sign or belong to a wolf clan have this trait as part of their spirit.

The wolf also symbolizes loyalty, importance of family and protection of others and is a skilled communicator. People who have the wolf as a spirit animal possess many of these qualities. The wolf is deeply connected to the moon and avoids confrontation. However, if attacked, the wolf will fight back.

People who have the wolf as a spirit animal or totem feel uncomfortable with those who do not freely communicate how they feel. If someone intellectualizes too much, then a wolf can become impatient with such a person.

If you come across a wolf in your life, be it in the physical world, in a dream or during mediation or a spirit journey, it can mean that it is time for you to become a teacher, either to yourself or someone else. It is time to trust your instincts or your inner voice instead of the voices of others or those who claim to be teachers or guides.

The appearance of the wolf suggests that even though you may be feeling out of sorts or are in some kind of danger, you are being protected by those close to you or those who love you the most.

If you're feeling lost in any way, whether in a relationship, in a job or in some other area of your life, it is a good time to ask for the wolf's help as a spirit animal. The wolf can be a useful guide to get you back on your true path. Wolf totems help you to discover whether someone is speaking the truth from their heart and not just their head.

One way of calling on the power of the wolf is to relate a personal story about yourself to one person or a small group of people. Your expressions and body language should be more pronounced while you tell this story in order to clearly communicate your thoughts.

You can also call on the wolf by simply showing members of your family that you love them, either through your actions or words. Or both.

And finally, one of the best ways to call the wolf into your life is to allow yourself to be a little bit wild. Go on an adventure, and do something out of the ordinary. Or simply go outside on a night with a bright moon (full or not) and howl. You may be surprised by the response you get, not just from yourself but from others.

WATER

Beaver

BEAVERS WERE WIDESPREAD across North America for millennia, which is why many Native peoples are familiar with these animals. The beaver is a common clan animal for many nations, including the Ojibwa, the Abenaki, the Huron, the Iroquois in the east, the Muskogee Creek, the Caddo and the Mojave in the south, and the Tlingit and the Kwakiutl along the northwest coast of the Pacific. The beaver is important to the Pacific Coast people, and its image is often seen on totem poles.

Beavers are semi-nocturnal, semi-aquatic animals that live in small family colonies. They are herbivores, their diet consisting of water lilies, leaves, bark, twigs and roots.

The average beaver weighs 24 to 66 pounds with a body length of between 31 and 47 inches, not including the tail. The tail, which can be 10 to 20 inches long, is one of the most distinct features of the animal. It is wide and flat, like a canoe paddle, and scaly; it helps the animal swim. Beavers use their tail to pat down mud when building dams and lodges. They also bang their tales against the water, creating a loud slapping noise to warn of predators or scare off interlopers.

Beavers are one of the most important animals in the area in which they live because they help in creating a habitat that countless other creatures use. They design and build dams out of trees, branches and mud, and these dams can block off a stream and create a large reservoir of water that becomes the main habitat of the beaver colony. Beavers construct large living spaces, their main residence, in the middle of this reservoir. And so the beaver's home is protected from predators by a large body of water. The entrance to the lodge is underwater, providing the animals with even more protection.

Beavers also excavate canals through areas that are too shallow or full of weeds so they can transport the materials needed to build and maintain their dams and lodges. All of structures that the beavers build require maintenance and repair, so beavers are constantly working. The dam beavers build also acts as a natural filter, removing silt and pollutants from waterways. The beaver's logging of trees opens up the forest floor, allowing the growth of underbrush, which attracts other animals like deer, moose and other large herbivores and their predators. Even when beavers leave an area, following the natural collapse of the dam after a few generations, their impact is still felt. An abandoned beaver pond usually transforms into a meadow, an open area that several years earlier was just a stream through a thick forest.

No other animal, besides humans, changes their landscape to the scope of what the beavers accomplish. Because of the beaver's ability to build and change their habitat, many Native cultures see the animals as representatives of hard work, industry and perseverance. To some cultures, the beaver is a smart creature with strong family connections, a cultural hero that uses its wisdom and industry to defeat evil and transform the world for the greater good.

To the Blackfoot of southern Alberta and northern Montana, the beaver is a creature of wisdom and the animal that gave the people the gift of tobacco, as described in the following story.

The Beaver and the Sacred Herb

Once there were four brothers, four medicine men who had strong spiritual powers. One day, the eldest had a vision, a voice that said to him, "There is a sacred herb. Pick some and burn it."

The eldest brother did as he was told, and he noticed that the smoke from the burning herb had a pleasant scent.

The second brother then had a vision of this herb. He was told to chop the herb and to carry it in a pouch made out of animal hide. He did this, and the scent it gave off was pleasant.

The third brother's vision told him to make a pipe out of bone. He made four pipes, gave three to his brothers and kept one for himself.

The youngest brother finally had a vision, too. He was told to put the herb into the pipe, set it on fire and inhale the smoke. He was also told to sing songs and pray while he and his brothers smoked the pipe. And they did, marking the first time that men ever smoked *nawakosis* (tobacco) together.

All the brothers had another vision, which was to share the herb and ritual with all the other people. But they thought it was too good to share with the common people, so they kept the herb a secret. They planted the herb in secret places and sang their songs far away from others. Since *nawakosis* was meant to calm the spirit and bring peace, health and unity, a war ensued and disease spread among the people because the brothers did not share the herb.

But a man named Bull-By-Himself knew that the brothers were up to something, and he did not like it. He decided that he was going to find *nawakosis* and learn how to plant and grow it, so that everyone could enjoy it.

Bull-By-Himself and his wife set up a lodge near sacred waters. For days, Bull-By-Himself went in search of the herb, but the only thing he found was food.

One day, while Bull-By-Himself was searching, his wife heard singing. She looked all around but could see nothing. Except for some beavers across the lake. When her husband returned, she told him about the songs.

"You are imagining things," he said.

"No, I'm not," his wife replied. "I can hear it now."

Bull-By-Himself could hear nothing. His wife realized that the beavers were singing. She went to the beaver lodge and ripped a hole in the lodge. The animals were dancing and singing.

"Close the hole you made!" said the beavers. "It is cold!"

"I will if you teach me your song and share your medicine with me," said the woman.

"Okay. Tonight we will come and visit you at your lodge," said the beavers.

The woman fixed the hole and went back to the lodge. At night, the beavers came. As soon as they stepped into Bull-By-Himself's lodge, they turned into four men.

"Why have you come here?" one of the beaver men asked.

"I have come to find *nawakosis*," said Bull-By-Himself. "Four men in our village know of its power but will not share it. I plan to share it with all the people."

"Then you are lucky to find us," said one of the beavers. "*Nawakosis* is great medicine, and we will share its secrets. But only if you promise to share it with all your people."

Bull-By-Himself and his wife agreed.

So the beavers taught the couple all the secrets of *nawakosis*. They showed them where to find the seeds, how to prepare them, where to plant them, how to care for the plants and when to harvest the leaves.

The beavers then taught the couple the songs and the dances for the *nawakosis*. When they shared all the secrets of *nawakosis*, the beaver men then turned back into beavers and swam away.

And that season, a great storm came and destroyed all of the *nawakosis* that the four greedy brothers had planted. They had not saved any seeds so they couldn't plant more.

Only the *nawakosis* planted by Bull-By-Himself and his wife survived the great storm. And they kept their promise to the beavers and shared it with anyone who would learn to smoke it in a sacred way.

Beavers are seen as stubborn creatures that work all the time without any other enjoyment. And these creatures build dams, flooding the world for their own sake, mindlessly destroying land used by other animals and humans. Beavers figure prominently in several stories about the world flooding. The following story features Wisagatcak, the Cree trickster Creator.

Wisagatcak and the Great Beaver

Not long after creating the world, Wisagatcak decided he wanted to capture the Great Beaver. So Wisagatcak built a giant dam across the river where the Great Beaver had its lodge.

"When the Great Beaver comes out," the trickster Wisagatcak said to himself, "I will attack him with a spear."

But the Great Beaver had strong magic, and just as Wisagatcak was about to throw the spear, the

Great Beaver cast a spell that caused a muskrat to bite the trickster on his behind. Screaming in pain and surprise, Wisagatcak missed his target, and the Great Beaver survived. Even so, the Great Beaver vowed revenge.

Over several days, the Great Beaver and all the little beavers built so many dams that the world began to flood. Wisagatcak destroyed the dam he had built, but nothing would stop the water from rising. Before the entire world flooded, Wisagatcak built a raft out of the remnants of his dam and invited as many animals as possible to stay on the raft.

For two weeks, the water rose. The muskrat swam away to find land but even though the muskrat was a skilled swimmer, he drowned. The raven flew around the entire world but didn't find a single piece of land.

Because of all the moisture in the air, moss grew on Wisagatcak's raft. He gave the moss to the wolf and told him to run around the raft. The wolf did so, and using his own magic, Wisagatcak caused the moss to expand until the earth was rebuilt.

Today, water still springs out from the earth, from the holes of the original raft.

The Beaver Wars

It should be noted that many Native cultures suffered because of the presence of the beaver.

When the Europeans arrived in North America after Christopher Columbus, they came looking for gold. Instead they found other items that became more lucrative than gold. The beaver pelt was one of those items.

From 1550 to 1850, hats made from beaver pelt were popular in Europe. The fur was soft yet durable, and a variety of hat styles could be made. Because of the popularity of these hats, beavers in Europe were hunted to near extinction.

When the Europeans came to North America, they realized there were seemingly countless beavers in the massive continent. The North American fur trade was established when Native peoples hunted the beavers in exchange for trade items. The fur trade, especially in beaver pelts, is considered a key factor in the European exploration and development of Canada. However, as happened in Europe, beavers in eastern Canada and the United States were hunted to near extinction because of the demand for their pelts.

In 1638, the Mohawk nation of eastern Canada and the United States, who were encouraged, backed and armed by the Dutch (and partly the English), moved against the Algonquin-speaking people such as the Ojibwa, the Huron and the Erie, among others, in order to gain control of the trade in beaver pelts. The French became involved in the conflict by fighting the Mohawks directly and arming and encouraging other nations to fight against the Mohawk nation.

Over the course of 70 years, from 1628 to 1701, the war over control of the fur trade raged on throughout the entire Great Lakes region. It is considered the longest and one of the bloodiest wars in North American history. The war resulted in countless deaths and the destruction of many Native societies. Much of the area along the Ohio River Valley south of Lake Erie remained unpopulated for more than half a century because the people had fled to escape the war.

Finding the Beaver

Because beavers are spread throughout North America, many Native peoples, from the Chippewa to the Creek, the Huron, Mohawk, Tlingit and Kwakiutl, among others, have beaver clans.

The Native American zodiac features the beaver as one of its signs. If you are born between April 20 and May 20, you are born under the sign of the beaver. A person with this sign is stubborn but methodical.

Because beavers are semi-aquatic animals, people who follow the beaver as a spirit guide have a strong love of water. In many cultures, water is connected to the spirit world so beavers are seen as good travelers in that realm. However, beavers cannot stay forever in that world and must come up for air.

Beavers also represent industry and handiwork. People with the beaver as a spirit guide or totem are always busy. But they never take on more than they can handle; they just do the work that needs to be done, which is usually ongoing. And because beavers mate for life, a person who follows the beaver as a spirit animal is considered to be family oriented and monogamous.

It should also be noted that those who are part of the beaver clan, who are born under the sign or who follow the beaver spirit animal can be stubborn and selfish to the point of obstinate. They always seem to be on task, constantly working and never taking time to enjoy the good things in life.

If you dream of a beaver or of a spirit that reminds you of a beaver, it may indicate that you tend to procrastinate. If you have a project that needs to be done, your only solution should be to get it done. Having a vision of a beaver means your home, your mind or your spirit is cluttered and you need to clear up the disorder in your life. You must become aware of doing tasks that are unimportant yet take up too much of your time and energy. The vision of a beaver also means you have a strong desire to bring your visions into fruition, and if you work hard, you will succeed.

Duck

THE DUCK IS A FUNNY-LOOKING animal, with a round body, an elongated neck and a flat bill. Ducks are good swimmers but ungainly on the land, waddling about on floppy webbed feet. They don't have the soaring majesty of the eagle, falcon or even the raven, but ducks can fly incredibly long distances, migrating thousands of miles every year between their winter and summer homes.

Ducks live everywhere on the planet except in Antarctica. There are over 120 species of ducks worldwide, a good number of them living in North America in its lakes, swamps and other bodies of water.

All North American ducks breed in the summer, usually in a more northern climate and then migrate south during the winter months. Though ducks are considered monogamous, most species bond just for a single year, and some duck pairs bond for several years.

During their annual breeding season, ducks prefer to nest in secluded areas near water and lay between 5 and 11 eggs. The female usually sits on the nest, protecting the eggs, which is why the female of many species has a plain color to camouflage itself. Male ducks on the other hand, such as the mallard with its bottle-green head and iridescent blue underwing feathers, are sometimes brightly colored.

Because ducks are prey for foxes, wolves and other animals as well as humans, they are not seen as a major spirit animal. In much of Native folklore, ducks are seen as gullible creatures, continually conned and fooled by tricksters such as the coyote, wolverine and fox. Despite their gullibility, ducks do deserve some respect.

This Blackfoot story tells how the ducks became colorful.

How Ducks Got Their Bright Colors

If you have seen the Duck people, you will notice that they wear brightly colored clothes. But most people don't know the reason behind this.

One fall, a long time ago, the Duck people were getting ready to fly away for the winter like they always do. On the lake, an old man was watching the Duck people, and he noticed that they all had the same colors. The old man gathered a large ball of green moss and carried it to the edge of the lake. The Duck people saw him and backed away, moving to the middle of the lake where it was safer. They knew the old man liked to play tricks.

The old man built a lodge with long poles and covered it with his big ball of moss. "Come, my brothers," he said to the Duck people. "I want to give you a dance, so come join me in my new lodge."

"Don't listen to him," said the geese to the ducks. "He's planning something bad."

The old man built a fire in his lodge and started singing a song in Duck language, and it was pleasing to the ducks. They swam to the shore and waddled closer to the old man's lodge to hear the song better. The Duck people and other birds such as the loons and geese were wary of trouble, but the old man sang so wonderfully that the birds became entranced with the music and walked right into his lodge.

The loon stopped near the door because he knew the old man was up to something. The goose stayed back as well. But all the ducks gathered around the fire in the lodge.

"First we all must be painted in different colors," said the old man. "Mallard, you will be first. What color do you want to be?"

"Paint my head green, put a white necklace around my neck and give me a brown breast and yellow legs," said the mallard. "But don't paint my wife that way."

So the old man painted the mallard the way the bird asked. And then he painted all the other ducks the way they asked.

Once all the ducks were painted, the old man said, "Now we are going to do a blind dance, and you will have to close your eyes. But no peeking. If you peek, you will have sore eyes forever."

The ducks shut their eyes as the old man began to sing. The Duck people began to dance around the fire, but the old man didn't care. The goose was correct; it was a trick. Once the Duck people were tired from all the dancing, the old man grabbed them so he could eat them.

But the loon peeked, and he saw the old man reaching for the mallard.

"Look out!" cried the loon. "He wants to kill us all! Everyone fly away!"

And all the birds flew away, with a lot of quacking and squawking and flying feathers. They escaped from the old man.

The old man was so angry that before the loon could fly away, he kicked the bird in the back, twisting the loon's legs. Which is why the loon has funny-looking feet. Also, the loon and all the other birds that peeked at the old man that night had sore red eyes.

All the Duck people had escaped from the old man, but they couldn't wash off the paint, which is why they all have those colors to this day.

The ducks escaped in this story, but usually the birds are captured and eaten because of their gullibility. However, in Native cultures in the northeast United States, the duck is seen differently. The duck in this region of North America is a nobler creature, a hero to many.

In a few northeastern Native cultures, it is the duck, not the muskrat, that is the earth diver creature—the animal that dives to the bottom of the ocean after the great flood to bring up mud for the Creator to rebuild the world.

In the Ojibwa culture, an underdog hero called Shingebiss is a character in many stories. In a few of these stories, Shingebiss is depicted as a young woman. The Ojibwa honored the duck as a resilient creature, so more commonly, Shingebiss is depicted as a hero duck, as in the following story.

Shingebiss and Spirit of the North

Shingebiss was a resourceful duck that lived in a lodge by a lake. She spent her days doing all the things ducks did—swimming in the lake and catching fish. One cold winter, Shingebiss stayed behind, unlike the other ducks that flew south for the winter.

At that time, the Ojibwa also left the area for the winter because it was too cold, and there was not enough food for them to eat.

But not Shingebiss. When the lake froze, she cut a small whole in the ice to catch fish. She lit a fire in her lodge to keep warm.

Kabibona'kan, the Spirit of the North and the maker of winter, saw the duck living her life, unaffected by the cold and ice. Kabibona'kan was annoyed with the bird because the cold and the ice didn't bother her, and he wanted to teach Shingebiss a lesson. So the Spirit of the North made the weather 10 times colder and sent 10 times more snow to freeze the duck out and force Shingebiss to fly south for the winter.

Shingebiss was not affected by the colder weather; she continued to fish in the hole in the ice and live in her warm lodge with a fire.

Kabibona'kan decided that he would visit Shingebiss' lodge. He thought that his mere presence in the lodge would freeze the little duck out. But when Kabibona'kan entered the lodge, Shingebiss just built up her fire more.

Kabibona'kan began to notice that his headdress of icicles was drooping. His clothes of ice and snow were becoming soggy and full of holes. Drops of water ran down his face. He first thought he was crying, but he knew he didn't cry. He realized that he was melting, and if he didn't leave the lodge, he would melt to nothing.

The Spirit of the North figured that Shingebiss had powerful medicine and decided to leave her alone. He left the lodge and gave up trying to freeze out Shingebiss.

In the spring, the ducks returned and were surprised to find Shingebiss alive.

And though the ducks still head south for the winter, the Ojibwa no longer do. Shingebiss taught them all the ways to stay warm and the ways to find food in the winter.

Finding the Duck

Despite not being considered a major spirit animal by most Native cultures, a number of peoples have duck clans, such as the Chippewa, the Menominee of Wisconsin and the Caddo.

If you are of a duck clan or follow the duck as your spirit animal, you prefer to stay around your home, your "nest," and keep it safe. You are generous, have a big heart and love to be around others, especially those who have the same temperament and outlook on life. Ducks are also resilient.

Obviously, if the duck is your spirit animal, you love the water and can swim effortlessly. A duck's ability to appear calm on the surface of the water while paddling underneath, along with being able to dive beneath the surface are symbols of the ability to travel easily in your subconscious. This skill allows you to build a stronger emotional balance that you can access during times of hardship.

You can call on the duck spirit animal when you are in need of emotional strength or when you're entering a new cycle in your life.

And if a duck shows up in your life either through dreams or if you encounter the bird in real life, you are reaching a time of fertility, either in the physical world or through your emotions or creativity. The duck signifies that you should not deny yourself emotional and physical comfort. And finally, if you follow the duck animal spirit, you understand that life shouldn't be viewed so seriously. A duck knows that it is wonderful to play and laugh, especially at oneself.

Muskrat

OUT OF ALL THE SPIRIT animals discussed in this book, the muskrat is probably the most underrated. Although many New Age books on animal spirit guides or Native animal symbols barely mention the muskrat, and in some cases ignore the animal completely, the muskrat is a significant animal to many Native cultures. The Ojibwa, Mohawk, Cree, Odawa, Potawatomi, Iroquois, Algonquin, Abenaki, Blackfoot and almost every Native group that lives or lived in the habitat of the muskrat sees this small beaver-like mammal as a major spirit animal.

Various peoples had different names for this animal. The Abenaki used *moskaws* for the muskrat; in Powhatan it was *musscasus*; in Lenape it was *temuskwus*; in Ojibwa stories it's known as *wa-zhushk*.

When Europeans first came to North America and encountered the muskrat, they referred to it as musquash, which they said was what the local Algonquians called it. However, because the animal had a long, thick tail, it reminded Europeans of a rat, so they combined the word "musquash" with the more familiar "rat," and the term "muskrat" was born.

Although muskrats are from the rodent family, they resemble a vole or a lemming rather than a rat. Weighing between 1.5 and 4 pounds with a body length of 9 to 13 inches, muskrats are about four times larger than the average rat and about one-quarter the size of an average-sized beaver.

Like the beaver, muskrats are nocturnal animals and spend much of their time swimming in water. Their habitat ranges from the Atlantic Coast to the Pacific, including much of North America from southern Alaska to Florida, and parts of California to the Maritimes. Depending on the habitat in which they live, muskrats build their homes out of plant stems and mud or live in burrows dug directly into the banks of rivers. The lodges are usually rebuilt every year. The entrances of both types of homes are positioned well below the waterline so that when water levels are low, they aren't exposed. Also, the entrances are built below the waterline so that when the water freezes, the muskrats are still able to enter or leave their homes. Because of this, muskrats only live in bodies of water that don't freeze all the way to the bottom.

Muskrats that live near the Arctic where lakes and streams are frozen for much of the year create shelters of stems and mud over the tops of holes in the ice.

Because those muskrats need a layer of snow over the lodges to help keep them warm and to prevent their entrances from freezing, many Native societies use muskrats to predict winter snowfall. If the muskrats start building big lodges long before the expected time of freeze-up (usually late September to early October depending on the part of the continent), it is considered a predictor of a winter with light snowfall. The reasoning is that a bigger lodge needs less snow as insulation during the cold weather. However, if the muskrat starts building a small lodge after freeze-up, it was a predictor of a winter with heavy snowfall.

Many Native groups, including the Nipmuc people of New England, built their homes in the shape of a dome, an idea they borrowed from the muskrat. After the world was created, says one story, the muskrat made its home round, in the shape of the world, and used the same materials that were used to make the world: plants, branches and mud. The people built their homes in a similar way.

Because they can build their own homes, as well as predict the type of winter that will come, muskrats are seen as being wise, well-organized and fastidious creatures. A person who dreams of muskrats is seen to be in need of eliminating clutter, be it physical clutter into their homes or emotional clutter in their lives.

But since muskrats are small rodents, rarely seen during the day, they are also incorrectly seen as unimportant creatures. This attitude is sometimes reflected in the stories in which the muskrat plays a key role. In these stories, the muskrat is seen as a small and insignificant animal, one to be fooled or not to be taken seriously. But appearances can be deceiving as indicated in the following Lakota tale.

Iktomi and the Muskrat

Iktomi was a trickster and mischief-making character, normally taking the shape of a spider-like creature. But since he was a shape shifter, he could assume any shape, including that of a human.

The trickster was sitting by a lake about to enjoy a pot of boiled fish. Since Iktomi had no regular mealtimes, he was hungry at all times of the day. Not knowing when his next meal would be, he had hoped to eat all the fish so it would last him a while.

But before he could start to eat, he heard a voice from the tall reeds.

"Hello, hello, my friend," said the voice.

Iktomi first thought it was the wild rice talking to him, but then a muskrat, dripping wet, came out of the reeds.

"Oh, it is you. Hello, my friend," Iktomi said to the muskrat.

The muskrat, too, was hungry, but he waited quietly until he was invited to enjoy the meal with Iktomi. The muskrat didn't expect to wait long because, as per Lakota tradition, Iktomi was supposed to say something like, "Be seated beside me, my friend. Let me share my food with you."

But Iktomi was hungry and didn't feel like sharing his food. He wanted the whole meal to himself. After an awkward moment, he came up with a plan.

"Let's run a race, and the winner will get this pot of fish," said Iktomi. "If I win, I will not have to share with you. But if you win, you may have half of it." Iktomi stood up, tightening his belt, ready to run.

"But I cannot race you," said the muskrat. "My legs are short, and I am not a swift runner. Your legs are long, and you are as a nimble as a deer."

Iktomi agreed and looked about for a moment. The muskrat saw that the trickster was hatching some kind of plot, so he realized he had to proceed carefully.

"I know," Iktomi said, his eyes brightening with an idea. "I'll carry a rock on my back. That will weigh me down, slow my speed so the race will be a fair one."

The muskrat agreed, and together they found a large rock on the other side of the lake, half buried beneath the mud. Iktomi wrapped the rock in a blanket, and with the muskrat's help, heaved the rock onto his back.

"Now whoever runs back to the other side of the lake to the pot, wins," Iktomi said. "And the winner shall get the fish."

They raced, and even though the rock was heavy, Iktomi felt he could still beat the muskrat. What the muskrat said was true; his legs were short, and he couldn't run fast. As he ran, Iktomi looked for the muskrat or for any sign of the muskrat in the reeds. But he saw nothing.

Iktomi thought he must be beating the muskrat, but he saw nothing behind him. The rock was getting heavy, and the effort to carry it caused sweat to pour down his face and his chest to heave with deep breaths.

"Enough," he said, flinging the rock off his back. He ran quickly to his goal, the pot of boiled fish. But when he arrived, he suddenly stopped, as if he had run into an invisible wall. The pot and the fish were gone. The muskrat was nowhere to be seen.

"Oh no, he must have run under the water, as fast as a flying arrow and laughed at me while I carried my heavy stone," said Iktomi with dismay. "If only I had shared my food like a real Lakota, I would not have lost it all."

Iktomi stumbled to the edge of the water and looked out. The muskrat was at his lodge, eating the fish. The muskrat laughed when he saw Iktomi.

"Please, please. I am hungry," begged Iktomi. "At least give me a fish bone to eat."

So the muskrat tossed a small bone to Iktomi. The trickster opened his mouth wide to catch it but almost choked to death before he could get it out.

The muskrat only laughed at him. "Next time, say to a visitor, 'Be my friend, sit beside me and share my food.'"

A few other stories are similar to this one, but the major story featuring the muskrat deals with the creation of the world. This creation story is told in many Native societies, including the Cree, Mohawk, Ojibwa and Potawatomi. The following story comes from the Ojibwa but most of the Native societies that lived on both sides of what is now the Canada/U.S border have a similar creation tale featuring the muskrat.

Creation of Turtle Island

Long ago, after the Great Mystery, the time when the world was first created, the first people of the earth, the Anishinaabe, began to stray from their harmonious ways. Brother turned against brother, and soon the people began to fight, argue and to kill one another over hunting grounds and other disputes. Seeing that harmony and respect for all living things was no longer on the earth, Kitchi-Manitou, the Creator, decided to flood the world in order to purify it.

The Mush-ko-be-wun, or Great Flood, destroyed the people, their homes and many of the animals as well. Only Nanaboozhoo (a trickster figure and Ojibwa cultural hero) managed to survive, along with a few other animals.

Nanaboozhoo clung to a log, searching for land. But he could find none. He allowed the surviving animals to take turns sitting on the log so they could rest from their constant swimming or flying.

After some time, Nanaboozhoo decided to do something. "I am going to swim to the bottom of the water and find some dirt of the old earth. With this new dirt, I believe we can create a new land for us to live on, with the help of the four winds and Kitchi-Manitou."

So Nanaboozhoo dove into the water and was gone a long time. When he finally surfaced, he was short of breath. After resting for a bit, he told the animals that the water was too deep for him to swim to the bottom to find the earth.

"I can dive under the water for a long time," said Mahng, the loon. "That is how I catch my food. I will try to make it to the bottom and return with some earth in my beak."

The loon dove and was also gone for a long time, much longer than Nanaboozhoo. Surely, the loon must have drowned, the others thought.

But then the loon floated to the surface, weak and barely alive. "I couldn't make it," the loon said after catching his breath. "There must be no bottom to this water."

Then Zhing-gi-biss, the grebe, spoke up. "Everyone knows I can dive to great depths, even farther than the loon, so I will try."

The grebe, too, was gone for an even longer time, and again everyone thought he must have drowned. But then the grebe surfaced, unconscious. When the bird finally awoke some time later, he said he could not reach the bottom to get the dirt.

Other animals tried to reach the bottom, Zhongwayzh, the mink, and even Mi-zhee-kay, the turtle. All of them failed, and it seemed there was no way to reach the bottom of the water to get the dirt to remake the world.

Finally, when everyone thought all was lost, a small voice spoke. "I can reach the bottom."

Everyone turned to see who had spoken and at first, they couldn't see the animal. Finally, Wazhushk, the muskrat, stepped up.

"I'll try to reach the bottom and bring up the earth," said the muskrat.

Some of the larger, stronger animals laughed at the muskrat. If they couldn't reach the bottom, how could such a small creature?

Nanaboozhoo silenced the laughter. "Only Kitchi-Manitou can judge others," he said. "If the muskrat wants to try, he can."

So the muskrat dove into the water and was gone much longer than any of the other animals. Nanaboozhoo and the other animals were sure that the muskrat had drowned.

But below the surface of the water, the muskrat did reach the bottom and managed to grab a small amount of dirt. The water was very deep, and by this time, the muskrat was almost out of air. With all the energy he had left, the muskrat pushed off the bottom of the lake and swam for the surface.

A long time later, one of the animals spotted muskrat floating on the surface of the water. Nanaboozhoo pulled muskrat onto the log, but it was too late.

"Oh no, brothers and sisters," said Nanaboozhoo. "Muskrat went too long without air, and now he is dead."

The animals sang a song of mourning and praise, but as the muskrat's spirit passed onto the other world, Nanaboozhoo saw something. "Look, there is something in his paw."

Nanaboozhoo opened the muskrat's paw, and there in the middle of his little paw was a tiny amount of earth. Everyone shouted with joy, but also with sadness. Muskrat had sacrificed his life so they could rebuild the earth.

Because of their sacrifice, the muskrats that came after the world was rebuilt were given a good life; they had the freedom to swim in all the lakes, ponds, rivers and streams. Muskrats also remembered the great flood and the new earth that was created. They build their homes in water, which are shaped like a mound of dirt—the same shape and material of the earth. And no matter that the marshes have been drained and their homes destroyed, muskrats still thrive.

Without the skills and tenacity of the muskrat, the world would not have been built, and many of the peoples would not have learned how to build their homes.

Finding the Muskrat

Even though the muskrat is one of the key animals in several Native creation stories across North America, there is not much literature on it in animal spirit guides. In fact, it is quite rare to find a book on Native animals spirits that includes the muskrat.

The muskrat is not included in the Native zodiac. And few tribes have muskrat clans. However, in the complex Anishinaabe clan system that covers many of the Algonquin-speaking peoples of eastern Canada and the United States, the muskrat is classified into the Moozwaanowe group. This group of animals is charged with scouting, hunting and gathering. Other animals in this group include moose, deer, elk and smaller mammals, including the fox, mink, beaver, porcupine, rabbit and raccoon.

If the muskrat is your animal spirit or you are part of a muskrat clan, you are seen as industrious, a critical thinker and well organized. You have a strong desire to live near or along a large body of water and not surprisingly, you are a great swimmer and enjoy different types of water sports.

Muskrats are a bit obsessive when it comes to personal and creative tasks. When you are involved in such a task, you sometimes lose track of time and ignore the other people around you.

If a muskrat appears in your dreams or during mediation or a spiritual journey, it can mean that your life is getting too busy and noisy. It is time to clean up the clutter in your physical or emotional world, but start slowly, one room or one emotion at a time. A muskrat also means it is time for you to become more contemplative, to meditate on your life in order to restore your physical and emotional energy.

Calling on a muskrat spirit guide is good when you are overwhelmed with the world, or if something is bothering you, and you need to determine the source of your troubles.

The appearance of a muskrat should not be dismissed because it is a smaller animal or not considered as prominent as other spirit animals. As noted earlier, the muskrat has been taken for granted, in the real world and in myth, but to many Native cultures in North America, the muskrat is important because of its key role in the creation of the world.

Orca

THE ORCA, OR KILLER WHALE as it was once called, is an extremely powerful spirit animal, especially to Native people who live on the Pacific Coast. Orcas possess a unique combination of characteristics. First, they were food for many cultures and are highly respected animals like the buffalo was to the Natives of the Great Plains or the salmon was to those groups who depended on fish for survival.

Orca are social hunters. In fact, in several Pacific Coast cultures, the orca is called the sea wolf because of its success in hunting as a pack.

There is a story about a young man walking along a beach when he hears some wolves whining. He follows the sound and discovers two orphaned wolf cubs, which he raises to become adult wolves.

To thank him, one day the wolves left his lodge and went hunting in the water. The man found the wolves had captured a whale, providing the people with much meat and blubber.

Pleased with what they had done, the wolves hunted more and more whales until there were few whales left. Seeing such great waste, the One Above called upon the Thunder Beings, the Rains and the Fog so that the wolves would not be able to find any whales to kill. But there was such a large amount of meat and blubber that it began to go to waste.

Seeing the waste, the Creator became angry with the wolves, and to punish them, the Creator convinced Grandmother Ocean to create big waves to prevent the wolves from returning to the land. And so the wolves became creatures of the seas—the "sea wolf."

Orcas are the largest member of the dolphin family, heavily built creatures with distinctive black and white markings. Male orcas are between 17 and 30 feet in length, with a weight between 3 and 10 tons. Female orcas weigh in the lower range and are 15 to 25.5 feet long. Males can live up to 60 years in the wild, while females can live almost 90 years.

Along with the orca's distinctive coloring, another way people can differentiate an orca from a whale or a dolphin is by the orca's dorsal fin.

Tall and triangular, the dorsal fin of the average male orca can be about six feet high, taller than the average human. Female dorsal fins are much smaller and less triangular in shape. The orca's dorsal fin is so distinct that marine biologists use the markings on this fin to identify individual animals within a group.

Orcas will eat almost anything they can catch, from sea mammals to fish (including large sharks) and from squid to turtles and seabirds. Resident orcas have also been known to hunt land animals such as deer or moose when these animals swim between islands along the coast.

Orcas are at the top of the food chain in the ocean, with no natural predators save for humans. And despite their previously more common name, killer whale, there is no single recorded incident of an orca killing a human being.

Since orcas are in the dolphin family, they are also mammals. Even though they are great swimmers—the fastest mammal in the ocean with a maximum speed of 35 miles per hour—orcas must surface every so often in order to breathe.

Orcas are considered one of the most social animals on the planet, living in tight-knit family groups called pods. There are three types of pods, pretty much describing three types of orcas.

The first type is the largest of the pod groups, known as offshore orcas, and contains animals of up to 25 orcas and more. They prefer to spend much of their time in the open sea, away from the coast. Offshore orcas hunt in groups and prey upon a wide variety of animals, even other whales much larger than themselves. These orcas also tend to be noisy animals, constantly communicating with other members of the pod.

The second group of orcas is the transient orcas. These animals live in a pod with a maximum size of seven animals, and they roam over a wide area along coastal regions around the world and into the open sea. These orcas are quiet when hunting; they communicate much less than the other two types of pods. They prefer to sneak up on their prey, which consists of other sea mammals such as seals and sea lions.

The final group of orcas, the resident group, is probably the group that some Native peoples were more familiar with. These pods live in specific areas along the coastal regions, territories that have, in a sense, been in the family for generations. Resident orcas are more commonly seen along the northwest Pacific Coast of North America, but resident pods are also present in coastal areas around Alaska, Norway, the UK, Russia and Antarctica. Resident pods range from 5 animals to 25, and like the offshore orcas, they communicate loudly and frequently. Their diet mostly consists of fish and squid.

An orca pod is a complex social group. Only elephants and higher primates such as apes and humans have more complex societies. Orca pods are always matriarchal, the animals living with their mothers for their entire lives. These pods are also extremely stable, with no animal straying from the group for more than a few hours at a time. Some pods can have four generations of animals living together. Researchers have noted that there are regional differences in languages between different pods.

No doubt the orca's social structure, along with its great ability to hunt, and the fact that these animals breathe air, has resulted in the connection that the peoples of the Pacific Coast have with the orca.

To the Kwakwaka'wakw of northern Vancouver Island, the orca was the ruler of the oceans, and all the other sea mammals such as dolphins, seals and sea lions, were its subjects. The dolphins were the warriors, and the other animals were "slaves." The Kwakwaka'wakw along with the Nuu-chah-nulth also believed that orcas were the souls of dead chiefs who had gone to live in the sea.

According to the Haida people of Haida Gwaii (formerly the Queen Charlotte Islands), orcas were the most powerful animal in the oceans. And they only took on the form of an orca when they were living and hunting on the surface of the water. When they returned underwater, they took on human form, living in houses and villages under the water. The Haida also believed any person who drowned went to live in these villages and would return now and again in the body of an orca to communicate and connect with their loved ones still living on land.

In the following Haida story, a man enlists the help of orcas to find his wife.

The Black Canoe

One day a man married a high-caste woman. He took his new wife to a bay where he knew there were orcas he could hunt. On their trip, they spotted an encampment with a tall fire blazing in the middle.

The man and his wife thought it was a camp of humans, but it was really a camp of orcas that had come ashore as they sometimes could. They even looked like humans.

As the couple got closer to the camp, the orcas realized that humans were on the way, and when the man and his wife arrived at the camp, they saw no one. The orcas had gone back into the ocean and left behind all their food.

"We are lucky to have found this," said the wife.

"Let us cook some, my wife," said the man. They cooked and ate a lot of the food. While they were eating, the wife looked out over the bay and saw something. It was a black canoe.

"Hold on, Husband. We should stop eating until this canoe comes," said the wife. "And then we can invite them to join us." The husband agreed.

The couple did not know that the canoe was actually a young orca disguised as a canoe. And all the other orcas that had been on the beach earlier were swimming under the water so the humans could not see them.

When the orca/canoe reached land, all the other orcas jumped out of the water, grabbed the man's wife and took her into the sea. They did this because the humans had taken their provisions without asking.

As the orcas rushed away with the woman, the man jumped in his canoe to chase them. But when they came to a deep part of the bay, the orcas dived down under the water and could no longer be seen.

Fortunately, there was a high cliff near this deep area. So the man climbed the cliff, filled his shirt with rocks and tied a long branch to his head and one on his back. He jumped off the cliff into the water, the rocks pulling him down to the bottom. He was hoping to use the branches to bring him up again once he found his wife. When he looked about, he realized that he was in the town of the sharks. And when he found the chief of the sharks, the fish recognized him. A long time ago, the man had tried to catch that shark, and they had a great battle. But since the shark had almost pulled his canoe over, the man had cut the line, letting the shark go free. The chief of the sharks respected the man as a great warrior and decided not to eat him. The shark decided he would help the man get his wife back from the orca village.

The sharks told him about a slave the orcas had. This slave owned the only stone axe in the village and would use it to cut wood for the fire in the house of the chief of the orcas. The chief of the sharks gave the man some medicine. "When you see the slave chopping wood, say to yourself, 'I wish your ax to break.'"

The man did what he was told, and the ax did break. The slave was upset because it was the only ax in the village. And if he couldn't chop wood for the fire, then the chief of the orcas would be angry with him. The man said he could fix the slave's ax, but for a price. If the man helped the slave, the slave would help the man rescue his wife.

"I am responsible for starting the fire in the house," the slave said, "and for collecting the water. Come by tonight, and I will knock over the fire. I will then pour water on it, and when steam rises, it will create a fog, and you can come in and steal your wife back."

The man was pleased, but the sharks had another reason for helping the man. They wanted to use the confusion to attack the orcas. So when the slave poured water on the fire to cause steam, the man tried to rush in, but the sharks went ahead of him. There was a great battle between the sharks and the orcas.

In the confusion, the man rushed in and found his wife. He grabbed her hand and dumped the rocks off his body, and the two of them rose to the surface of the water with the help of the branches on his head and back.

Afterwards, the couple learned that whenever the orcas left something on the shore for them, they would offer the proper thanks before they took anything.

The following story from the Tlingit tells of how the orcas came to be.

Natsilane the Carver

Long ago there was a skilled hunter and wood carver named Natsilane. He married the daughter of a chief from a nearby island. When Natsilane moved to his new wife's island to live with her family, at first he was accepted into the new clan and received great honor for his hunting and carving talents. However, his new brothers-in-law were jealous of the hunter and decided to get revenge on him.

During a seal hunt one day, Natsilane jumped out of a canoe to stab a sea lion on the rocks. But his spear broke, and the sea lion escaped into the water. Natsilane turned around to get back into the canoe but saw that his brothers-in-law were paddling away. They had planned to abandon him on the rocky island with no food or water.

Natsilane waited for a long time to see if anybody would come to rescue him, but no one did. So he fell asleep.

The next day, the hunter awoke to the sound of someone calling his name. He thought it was his rescuers and jumped up to greet them. Instead it was a huge sea lion that looked a little like a man.

"My son was injured by a human spear, and we cannot get it out to save him," the sea lion said. "Can you help us?"

Natsilane said he would try, and the sea lion asked him to follow him to the bottom of the ocean. Natsilane wasn't sure if he could survive under the water but realized he would probably die on the rock island anyway, so he followed the sea lion down to his village under the water.

The hunter was taken to the finest house in the village, and he realized that the sea lion was the chief of the other sea lions. In the house was a young injured sea lion, a spear sticking out of him.

Natsilane saw that the young sea lion was the one he had injured before he had been stranded on the island of rock. And because the spear was his, Natsilane was able to remove it and help heal the young sea lion.

The chief of the sea lions was pleased. He gave Natsilane some magic to improve his carving skills and then took him back to his village where the hunter was reunited with his wife. He told her what had happened.

"My brothers told me you had died in the water," she said.

"They lied because they were jealous of me," he said and asked her to keep his return a secret.

Before the sun rose the next day, Natsilane snuck out of the village and went into the woods with his carving tools. For a long time, he worked on his carving. And finally, he got it right, carving a huge black fish out of some special spruce he had found. He carved several more fish, and when he put them in the water, they came to life.

Because he was their creator, the black fish asked him what they could do for him. Natsilane told them to find his brothers-in-law and sink their canoe so they would drown. The fish did as they were told, but one of the brothers survived the attack, returned to his village and told the people the story about these new black fish that were bigger and faster than anything he had ever seen.

The people of the village were sad about the death of the brothers, so Natsilane told the black fish that they should never harm any humans, and they still listen to him.

And every so often, the black fish, orcas, show respect to Natsilane by leaving a freshly killed seal or other fish near the shore for the people to eat. The descendants of Natsilane still use the image of the orca as their crest.

Finding the Orca

Orcas are strong, intelligent creatures and great hunters with the ability to live above and below the surface of the ocean. And as such, the people living along the Pacific Coast consider these animals to be strong medicine, and resident pods have lived and hunted in the same region for centuries.

Orcas are considered guardians of the earth with great medicine for healing. And if you are of the orca clan or follow the orca as a spirit animal, you sense that you must protect the earth and help heal others, whether in body, mind or spirit.

Orcas mate for life and stay in large family groups for all of their lives, so if you are part of the orca clan or follow the orca as an animal spirit, family is one of the most important aspects of your life. Socializing with others, especially those closest to you, is key to your life. And when you make a connection with someone, be it a partner or friend, that connection is lifelong. The orca also teaches valuable lessons in communication, leadership and teamwork.

And because orcas are matriarchal, the animal spirit has a deep connection with the mother spirit, the feminine side and the earth itself. This is not to be taken as a weakness because the orca is a creature of great power, an apex hunter that will prey upon any creature, including the powerful polar bear and moose.

Only man is not considered a prey animal, and to many, this shows intelligence of the animal, and like the wolf, a deep kinship with humanity. The strength of the orca is quite balanced and controlled, but the animal is still wild at heart, a carefree spirit not held by the bounds of land and earth.

Orcas move between the surface of the ocean and what lies below, signifying the ability to travel easily between the material world and the spirit world. Individuals who follow the orca as an animal spirit have an affinity with the spirit world. That phase of existence is a welcoming and warm place for the orca, almost a second home. But since orcas need to breathe oxygen, they must return to the surface of the water to replenish their strength, or they will die.

This return to the surface is seen as a positive event, not a limiting one. And that's why orcas will sometimes breach the water, throwing their entire body up into the air as a celebration of this return.

If you encounter an orca in the water, it is a sign of good fortune. However, seeing an orca (or a whale) moving up a freshwater source can be an omen of negative things to come, and you must prepare for that day. Any image of an orca beaching itself is also a negative sign. You must work hard to allow that orca to return to the water in order to be free again.

Overall, the orca is a positive animal spirit, and its appearance means good things. It shows that you are surrounded by good friends and family who will help you to reach your goals if you call on them. The orca may be a sign to call on that help.

The orca animal spirit can also allow you to gain more intuition when communicating with others. Because the orca symbolizes teamwork and leadership, it may signal that it's time for you to step forward and work to get everyone on the same page in order to reach your target.

If you are feeling alone or require the support of those close to you, especially family, it might be wise to seek the orca animal spirit. The spirit can assist you in healing yourself and others and bring stability to those, including yourself, who are feeling out of sorts or unbalanced.

A good way to call on the orca is to sit in a quiet place near some water, possibly even a bath or a pool. Take a deep breath and hold it for as long as possible without harming yourself or causing light-headedness. Then breathe out and feel the tension release. Then revel in the next breath, in the life-giving oxygen and repeat the steps a few more times.

A trip to the coast, especially to a region where orcas live, is another way to connect with these wonderful creatures. If that's not possible, find a body of water nearby, not a river but a lake or pond, and sit quietly, breathing in and out, imagining yourself moving in and out of the water. Listening to the sound of orcas on headphones can also be calming.

The orca is a guardian and an intuitive animal that will watch over you. The medicine the orca offers is strong, but at no time will it overpower you like some spirit animals. This animal spirit is social and wishes to work with you to help you find your way.

Salmon

SALMON ARE AN IMPORTANT animal for the people who live on the Pacific West Coast. To these people, and in some cases also people from the Atlantic Coast, salmon was one of their primary sources of food. In spirituality, the salmon, like other animals, willingly give themselves up as food for humans.

Because salmon are extremely valuable to the survival of some cultures, there are also many highly specific ceremonies, rules and taboos associated with the fish. The most common ceremony is the first salmon ceremony. The point of this ceremony was to properly welcome the salmon back from their run. In the ceremony, the chief selects one of the fishermen from the village to be the first person to catch the first salmon. The first salmon had to be caught and filleted in a certain way, and the techniques varied from culture to culture. The fish was then divided among the respected people of the village. There were rules pertaining to which person ate a raw piece of salmon and which people were given a cooked piece of fish.

Sometimes the head of the salmon was put back into the river with its head pointed upstream in order to show the rest of the salmon which way to go during the run. All of the bones of the first salmon were carefully cleaned and placed back into the water to show respect. None of the meat was shared with the dogs in the village.

The steps of the first salmon ceremony had to be done precisely and in the correct order to show respect for the salmon (and the Salmon King or Chief) so that the fish would continue to offer themselves to the people as food. If the salmon were displeased in any way, they wouldn't return when they were expected. Or they wouldn't return at all.

Many peoples believed that the salmon were immortal, supernatural creatures that lived as humans on islands in the ocean or under the water in villages.

The Chinook people removed the heart of a salmon and burned it so that the spirit would not be defiled by dogs or wild animals consuming the heart, thus killing a future supply of fish. In times past, it was believed that anyone involved in the preparation of a corpse for burial might drive away the salmon, and as such, it is said that the people went so far as to bury the terminally ill while the person was still alive.

Salmon are migratory creatures that are also anadromous, meaning they are born in fresh water and then migrate to the ocean only to return to freshwater to spawn. During spawning, a female salmon will lay about 5000 eggs that are then fertilized by the male. These eggs become fry, which then mature into juvenile salmon, known as parr. The parr live in the freshwater river for six months to three years, depending on the species. It is believed only 10 percent of parr actually survive to the next stage of life, called smolt. The smolt make their way to the ocean where they spend the next one to four years at sea.

Once their time at sea is done, they return home, sometimes swimming hundreds of miles upstream to begin the process all over again. It is during this return trip that the fish are large and suitable enough to be caught. After spawning again, the adult salmon die.

Because of their unusual cycle of life, salmon are a keystone species for the people of the Pacific Northwest and Alaska. These fish are not only a food source for humans but also for birds and other animals, such as otters and bears, and how bears deal with salmon has a major effect on the forests of the Pacific Northwest.

Nearly half of the salmon that bears catch are left uneaten on the forest floor. The salmon that the bears do eat is also spread through the bear's urine and feces, which contain the nutrients of the salmon. It has been determined that almost one-quarter of the nitrogen provided to the forests of the Pacific Northwest comes from the salmon through bears.

Although folklore states that salmon will return to the exact location of their birth to spawn a new generation, this is not always true. The majority of salmon do return, but there are times when they do not. Environmental conditions in the river, the delta or the ocean may cause salmon not to return to the exact river or spot where they were spawned.

Sometimes salmon move or jump into different tributaries, and they spawn in new locations. Environmental conditions also may reduce the size of the salmon run. So while salmon are, for the most part, a reliable source of food, their numbers could fluctuate, and any changes in the salmon's habitat had major effects on the lives of the people who relied on them for food. This is one of the major reasons why the Native peoples had many ceremonies designed to show respect to this important fish. If the salmon run didn't go as well in previous years, the people were blamed, not the fish. Someone must have done something wrong to displease the salmon or the ceremonies weren't performed as well as they should have been.

There are many stories that show why the people developed these ceremonies in the first place, such as this story from the Squamish nation of British Columbia.

The Four Brothers

A long time ago, when humans and animals spoke the same language, there were four brothers who liked to help the people.

One day, the four brothers went to the Squamish people, and the chief asked them to stay. Knowing these brothers had some magic and liked to help, the chief asked them for a favor.

"Can you bring the salmon to our village?" asked the chief. "We are often short of food, and we know that the salmon are good, but they never come to our shores."

"We will talk to the salmon people and ask them," said the eldest brother. "We will ask Snookum, the sun, where they live."

After some struggle and trickery, the four brothers got the sun to tell them where to look for the salmon. "The home of the salmon is a long way off in that direction," said the sun, pointing toward the west. "If you want to visit them, you must first prepare much medicine and take it with you. Then all will be well."

And then the sun disappeared behind the clouds. The brothers collected the medicine according to the sun's instructions and went back to the Squamish people.

"Get all of your canoes and prepare for a long journey," said the eldest brother. "At sunrise, we will all leave to visit the salmon."

The next morning they started westward. They paddled for several days. Finally, they approached an island and saw what seemed to be a village near the shores. Smoke of all colors rose into the clouds.

"This looks like what we are looking for," said the brothers.

So the paddlers took the canoes to the beach, which was broad and smooth. All the Squamish people went toward the village, the four brothers carrying the medicine with them. They gave some of the medicine to Spring Salmon, the chief of the village, and he was friendly toward the whole party.

In the stream behind the village, Spring Salmon kept a fish trap. Shortly before the visitors had landed, the chief had directed four of his young people, two boys and two girls, to go into the water and swim up the creek into the salmon trap. Obeying his orders, the children had drawn their blankets up over their heads and walked into the sea. As soon as the water reached their faces, they became salmon. They leapt and played together, just as the salmon do in the running season, and frolicked their way toward the trap in the creek.

When the time came to welcome the strangers with a feast, the chief ordered others to go to the salmon trap, bring back the four fish they would find there, and clean and roast them for the guests. When the salmon were cooked, the chief invited his guests to eat.

"Eat all you wish, but do not throw away any of the bones," said the chief. "Be sure to lay them aside carefully. Do not destroy even a small bone."

The visitors did as they were asked. They ate the feast of salmon but wondered why they had to save the bones. When they were finished their meal, some of the young men from the village of the salmon people picked up all of the bones, took them to the beach and threw them into the sea.

Not long after, the four young people who had swum into the fish trap reappeared and joined the others. For four days, the salmon chief held feast after feast.

The way the salmon people handled the bones at each meal piqued the curiosity of one of the visitors. On the fourth day, he secretly kept back some of the bones and hid them. At the close of the meal, the rest of the salmon bones were collected in the usual manner and cast into the sea. Immediately afterwards, four young people came out of the white water. But one of them covered his face with his hands.

"Not all of the bones were collected. I do not have any for my cheeks and nose," said the young warrior.

"Some of the salmon bones are missing. Did any of you keep some of the salmon bones?" said the salmon chief.

Alarmed by this, the youth who kept his bones back pretended he had found some bones. The unfinished man was told to go back into the water. The chief threw the salmon bones in after the man, and the youth appeared, this time complete.

The Squamish finally knew that they had found the salmon people.

"We have come to visit you, salmon chief, for a special purpose," explained the oldest brother. "We came to ask you to allow some of your salmon people to visit Squamish waters. My friends are poor, and they often go hungry. We shall be grateful if your people will sometimes visit so they can be eaten."

"I will do as you request, on one condition," said the salmon chief. "They must throw all the bones back in the water as we have done. If you do this and are careful with the bones, my people can return home to us, after they visit and feed you. Do you promise?"

The Squamish and the four brothers all promised.

As they were leaving, the salmon chief said, "First, I will send Spring Salmon to you in the season. After them I will send the sockeye, then the coho, then the dog-salmon and last of all, the humpback."

And ever since that time long ago, the salmon have visited the Squamish in the order the salmon chief said they would. And the people were always careful with the bones, returning them to the sea.

Other peoples in North America, such as the Swampy Cree and those who lived near the Great Lakes, had other types of fish as a major part of their diet. But they didn't revere fish as deeply as the people of the Pacific Northwest revered salmon. Still, there are a number of fish-related stories, such as this short one from the western Great Lakes.

Why the Catfish Looks Like it Does

A long time ago, the catfish looked like a lot of other fish. But once, when the catfish were assembled in the water, an old chief said to them, "I have often seen a moose come to the edge of the water to eat grass. Let us watch for him and kill and eat him. He always comes when the sun is a little way up in the sky."

The catfish that heard what the old chief said and agreed to go and attack the moose. The big animals were scattered everywhere among the grass and rushes, but one moose came slowly along, picking grass. He waded into the water and began to feast. The catfish watched to see what their old chief would do, and presently one of them worked his way slowly through the grass to where the moose's leg was. The catfish thrust his spear into the moose's leg.

"Ouch! Something has stuck a spear into my leg," the moose said. And looking down, he saw the catfish.

The moose immediately began to trample all of the other catfish around him. Many of the catfish died, but some of them escaped, swimming down the river as fast as they could.

And while the catfish still carry spears in their mouths, they heads are still flat because they were trampled by the moose.

Finding the Salmon

Many inland Native cultures have fish as a clan, including the Ojibwa, the Creek, the Ho-Chunk and the Chickasaw. To almost every culture along the Pacific coast, the salmon is an important animal and figures in stories, ceremony and art, including totem poles and carvings.

The salmon is part of the Native American zodiac for those born between July 22 and August 21.

If you follow the salmon as a spirit animal, it is said you are resourceful, and people look to you for encouragement and counsel. You may listen to others and get advice and guidance but in the end, your own inner wisdom will be the major factor in decision-making.

And because salmon are known for finding their way back to their spawning grounds after years in the ocean, those who follow it as a spirit animal are excellent at finding their way. They also know what they want and how to achieve it, and they finish what they start, no matter the obstacles.

If you encounter a salmon, it could mean it's time to trust your gut and allow it to guide you to your destination. You may face many challenges in the future, but you will eventually find your way.

Finding or encountering a salmon may mean you will be called on to make some sort of sacrifice, but in the end, it will lead you to a rebirth of some sort. If you encounter many salmon, this is simply a sign for a time of plenty.

You may call on salmon in your visions or mediation if you're feeling lost in any way. Or if you feel you've lost purpose in life. The salmon helps get you back on track.

Salmon aren't vague creatures—their meanings are quite simple and straightforward.

Turtle

TURTLES, ESPECIALLY THOSE in North America, are relatively small, mostly shy animals that live quietly and spend a lot of time underwater. They aren't known for having great hunting skills, speed and agility, nor as creatures with power or strength. Because of the turtle's nature, the assumption is that it is not a strong spirit animal. But turtles have a special place in many Native American cultures.

From the Cree to the Blackfoot, from the Iroquois to the Lenape and other Native cultures, the turtle is a major character in their creation stories. Since this story was already told in the muskrat chapter, it won't be repeated in full.

But the basic story is that a great spirit built the world and all that was in it. For a long time, everyone lived in harmony. But soon, the humans began to argue among themselves and to disrespect the land, the trees, the waters and the animals. War raged. So the Great Spirit decided that a clean slate was needed and flooded the world.

How the world is flooded in creation stories varies. Sometimes beavers are involved, sometimes it rains for a long time or sometimes a lake or river overflows its banks and doesn't stop. No matter which way is described, the world is flooded, and all the humans and animals who can't swim or fly, drown.

Because the turtle can swim, it is one of the creatures that doesn't die in the flood. And because it has a hard shell and a broad back, it becomes a raft of sorts for those animals that survive the flood. The animals take turns floating on the turtle's back, resting for a moment from their swimming or flying, and then allowing another animal to take its turn. There is also a creator or other character in all of these stories. This character is not the Great Spirit but some kind of creature with magical powers, usually the cultural hero of the respective culture telling the story.

Using a diver character, the muskrat for the most part, but sometimes a duck, the cultural hero obtains a piece of mud from the bottom of the newly formed ocean. This piece of mud combined with a bit magic is used to rebuild the world on the back of the turtle. According to some groups, such as the Mohawk, earthquakes occur because the turtle is stretching its back because of the weight of the world.

The turtle's role in these stories is why many Native cultures, especially those in the northeastern part of the continent, around the Great lakes, the Cree and some Blackfoot, refer to North America as Turtle Island. Some Native peoples, Native rights activists and environmentalists use the term "Turtle Island" instead of "North America" to describe the continent, believing Turtle Island is its original name and should be adopted.

The place with the name "North America" is seen as a place that was undiscovered until 1492, and the term doesn't acknowledge that the continent was populated by a diverse group of cultures before that time. Using the term "Turtle Island" is said to better reflect the history of the continent.

Turtles are a group of reptiles, and the term is used to describe all types of turtles, regardless where they live. Some consider it more proper to call land turtles by the term "tortoise" and sea turtles as "turtles." However, the term "turtle" refers to both turtles and tortoises, especially since North America is known as Turtle Island not Tortoise Island.

Turtles are old animals; the earliest species of turtle lived over 215 million years ago, not long after the first dinosaurs evolved and 20 million years before the Jurassic period. Turtles were around almost 150 million years before T-Rex evolved.

Modern turtles can live for many years—over a century in some cases—but unlike most animals, their major organs do not deteriorate over time. And this fact has prompted many scientists to study turtles in an effort to improve the longevity of humans. The average turtle reaches sexual maturity in 10 years, but others may take up to 20 to 30 years to reach breeding age. But like their organs, their ability to breed does not decline as they age. However, turtles do not breed annually, but usually have a separation of some years between breeding cycles.

For the most part, turtles that live in North America, or rather, Turtle Island, are considered land turtles. Many of them live in aquatic environments such as rivers, lakes and swamps, but they must surface from time to time to breathe. However, many turtles can hold their breath for a long time—the length depends on the species, their size and what they are doing at the time. Hibernating turtles can stay underwater for months while other turtles that are not hibernating can stay underwater for more than an hour, and for others, it's only 15 minutes. And since turtles are cold blooded, their metabolism is much slower than a typical mammal, so they require less oxygen.

Many turtles in North America can travel on land, and although they move slowly, turtles are protected by the one characteristic that makes them different than any other reptile in the world—their shell.

The shell on most non-sea turtles is domed shaped and covers most of the turtle's body, in some cases, even the head. In other turtles, where the head isn't covered, they can pull their heads in for further protection. The turtle's shell is a type of modified boney structure that not only protects the animal from predators but can also be used as a means of identification either by the pattern on the shell, the shape of the shell, the type of shell or a combination of all three.

In this Ojibwa or Anishinaabe story, we find out how and why the turtle got its shell. This story features the Ojibwa cultural hero, Nanaboozhoo.

The Legend of the Turtle Shell

It was a day when Nanaboozhoo was feeling strange. Arguing blue jays had awoken him from a deep sleep. And not only was he cranky because of lack of sleep, but he was also hungry. So Nanaboozhoo went to the village to find something to eat. He came upon some men cooking fish. He asked for some fish, and the men gave him some.

"Watch out, Nanaboozhoo. The fish is hot," said the men.

But Nanaboozhoo did not listen to them. He grabbed the fish, and it burned his hand. He jumped up in pain and ran to the lake so he could put his hand in the water to cool it off. Because he was still groggy from being awakened by the blue jays, as Nanaboozhoo was running to the lake, he tripped on a rock. He fell on Mishekae, a female turtle, who was sunning herself on the beach. Back then, Mishekae did not have a shell. She was only made of soft skin and bone.

Mishekae screamed in pain and told Nanaboozhoo to watch where he was going.

Nanaboozhoo was ashamed that he had hurt the turtle because she was a nice creature and didn't bother anyone. He liked her. He apologized but then wondered, "What can I do to make it up to her?"

Nanaboozhoo thought about it for a while. But then he saw two large shells on the shore and took the shells to Mishekae. He put them together, picked up the turtle and put her in between them.

"There you go. Now you will never be injured again," he said. "And when danger comes, you can pull up your legs and your head to protect yourself."

Mishekae thought the shells were wonderful. She practiced sticking her feet, her head and her tail out of shell. Nanaboozhoo watched and realized something important.

"The shell itself is round like the Earth, and because you have four legs, each one will represent north, south, east and west," Nanaboozhoo said. "The people will see you, and you will give certain messages to them. When you draw your legs in, it will tell them that danger is near and all direction is lost. Your tail will show where they have been, and your head will show them where they should go.

"You will also be able to live in the water as well as on the land because you carry your house on your back."

Mishekae loved her new shell and thanked Nanaboozhoo for his wisdom. She pushed herself along the shore and disappeared into the water. And because Nanaboozhoo had shown her kindness after hurting her, the people see Mishekae as a special animal.

Other cultures, such as the Mik'maq and other Wabanaki people of eastern Canada, have a turtle character named Mikcheech who is more of a comic foil. Considered a harmless but buffoonish uncle,

Mikcheech appears in stories with Glooscap, the cultural hero of the Wabanaki stories. In this story, we see how Mikcheech becomes a turtle.

Mikcheech Gets Married

In the old time, there lived a Mik'maq named Mikcheech. He was an old, lazy bachelor who didn't take care of himself, and no one really paid any attention to him.

He wasn't smart, but he was cheerful, and Glooscap loved him for that.

One day, Glooscap transformed into a man and went to Mikcheech's lodge for a visit. Glooscap was treated as any guest should be treated—he was given a place near the fire and allowed to share in a delicious supper of fish.

After he was finished eating, Glooscap asked his old friend why he never married.

"I'm too lazy and old," Mikcheech said with a smile. "Who would marry me? I can't even clean or mend my own clothes."

"You need a wife to do that," said Glooscap, as he handed the old man his magic belt.

When Mikcheech put on the belt, he changed into a young, strong man dressed in fine clothing. The old bachelor was impressed with the magic.

"I can change your outside, but you have to change your inside," Glooscap said. "The rest is up to you."

Mikcheech realized that this was a trick to make him less lazy. But he smiled. "I see my easy times are over, and I must find a wife. But how long will this last?"

"As long as you are a man. Now there is a feast being held in the next village. Go find a wife."

Mikcheech went to the feast and saw the girl he wanted; she was the chief's youngest daughter and the most beautiful of the women.

It was the Mik'maq custom for a man to declare his love for a woman by throwing a chip of wood on her lap as he danced by. If she didn't like him, she would throw the chip over her shoulder. If she did like him, she threw the wood chip back to the interested party.

Much to Mikcheech's delight, the girl threw the wood chip back to him. He ran to the chief and said what a man was supposed to say when he wanted to get married: "I am tired of living alone."

"You are a brave man," said the chief, giving Mikcheech a strange look. "But you may have her as your wife."

Soon afterward, while the wedding feast was being prepared, Mikcheech went back to Glooscap to tell him the good news. But Glooscap did not look happy.

"All the young men in that village desired that girl," Glooscap said. "If you marry her, they will try to kill you."

Mikcheech wasn't a good warrior, but he still wanted to marry the chief's daughter. "What must I do?" he asked Glooscap.

Glooscap told Mikcheech that after the wedding feast there would be games. During the games, the young men would try to slay him by crowding him and trampling him to death. "When this happens, go and jump over your father-in-law's lodge to escape. Jump over it three times, and after the third time, you will become the chief of a new nation."

During the games after the wedding feast, the men of the village tried to kill Mikcheech, but he did what Glooscap told him—he jumped over the lodge three times. When Mikcheech landed after the third jump, his head turned green, his hands and feet became wrinkled and there appeared a hard shell on his back.

"What has Glooscap done to me?" Mikcheech said to himself.

The young men were surprised to see this new creature. But they knew it was still Mikcheech. They stabbed at him with their knives, but their knives couldn't penetrate the hard shell. They tried to cut off his head but Mikcheech pulled it into the shell.

The men then tried to burn him in the fire pit but they couldn't get the fire hot enough. So they threw him in the sea and left, thinking he would drown. The chief's daughter ran to the water's edge and wept for her lost bridegroom.

The next day, the young men saw something on a rock far out at sea. Thinking it was something good to eat, they took their boat and paddled over to it. When they reached the rock, they saw that it was Mikcheech, sunning himself.

Mikcheech laughed at the men. "I guess you can see I am enjoying my new home," he said. And then he dove into the water the way turtles do to escape danger.

The men realized that they had failed and had no power over Mikcheech.

And even though Mikcheech was safe, he was lonely.

"Oh, Glooscap. You promised I should have a wife and become chief over a new nation."

But then Mikcheech saw a green shape swimming toward him. It was another turtle, and he realized it was his new wife, the chief's daughter.

Over the years, Mikcheech and his wife had many children. And as promised by Glooscap, Mikcheech became the chief of a new nation, the nation of turtles.

Finding the Turtle

Because many Aboriginal people believe the world was built on the back of a turtle, this animal reflects much respect for Mother Earth and all she encompasses. The turtle represents peace with Mother Earth and peace among all of her inhabitants.

Many Natives peoples had turtle clans, too numerous to mention. The Wyandot people, also known as the Huron, had four separate turtle clans based on the four different species of turtles with which they had experiences. Other groups, such as the Lenape, have a turtle dance as part of their ceremonies.

If you follow the turtle as a spirit, you have a deep connection with Mother Earth. You may have hidden strength, something others may not notice, but at no time will you ever use that strength to harm the earth or to cause imbalance to an ecosystem.

And because of its connection to the earth, the turtle is a healer and protector. It is said that if a turtle appears in any form while someone is sick, either physically or emotionally, that person will not only be healed but will also live a long life.

In addition, singing songs and saying prayers to the turtle visitor will ensure faster healing. If no prayers are made to the turtle, the person will heal, but it will take longer.

Because turtles live a long time and can survive on land and in water, the animal signifies an ancient soul that moves easily into the spirit world. A turtle might move more slowly than most to connect to the spirit world, but once a turtle does, the connection is deeper than usual.

If you connect to the turtle spirit animal, you move at your own pace, not ignorant of others and their need, but with deliberation and focus. Most people will see that and, for the most part, will not attempt to rush you because they know you are on task and always deliver results.

The turtle may be a sign for you to slow down, to retreat for a moment and protect yourself or to take stock of the situation and your thoughts and emotions in order to regain balance. Relying on yourself instead of leaning on others is good idea when you encounter a turtle.

When you need to slow down, when you need to protect yourself or need time alone to reflect, these are the best times to call upon the turtle spirit. Change your daily routine, at least for a day, preferably more, to allow your natural rhythms to emerge. Do not plan anything or schedule what you should do or when you should meditate, pray or eat.

If there are too many demands on your time because of work, family or other obligations, then spend some time each day moving slower than usual. Walk slower between tasks or even just slow down your basic movements such as eating, picking up a fork and breathing. Expand this slowness to other areas in your life, and you may find yourself resetting the pace of your life to one that suits you better.

The turtle may be a funny-looking creature that is not seen much, moves a little slower and retreats when in danger, but it lives its own life, quietly and methodically doing what it needs to do, without feeling pressured from others to move faster. The turtle is one of the most honored creatures, not just by Aboriginal peoples but also by other cultures, such as the Chinese and Hindu who see the world being carried on a strong back.

And always remember, you do not live in North America; you live on Turtle Island.

Appendix

Native American Zodiac

IN THIS BOOK, THERE IS SOME mention of the Native American zodiac, although not all the animals in this zodiac are described.

First, it must be said that Native peoples had a great understanding of the movement of the stars, the moon, the planets, the sun and other astronomical phenomena. They used their knowledge of the heavens to predict such events as the coming of the solstices, the equinoxes and eclipses, as well as the changing of the new to the full moon, to name just a few. They also used their knowledge to note the changing of the seasons so they could prepare to plant their seeds or harvest their plants. Like many other cultures around the world, the sky was just another natural part of the planet, and the Native peoples of North America used the sky as one of their guides in life.

Many peoples also gave names to various constellations, planets and other sights in the night sky. Many Native cultures created medicine wheels, which are large, circular structures constructed out of stone that were used for astronomical purposes, as well as for ceremonies, healing and spiritual pursuits.

But even though Native Americans had great knowledge of the heavens, there wasn't a coherent collection of star signs, such as in the Western zodiac, which were consistent across the continent.

So the origin of the Native American zodiac is not entirely known. It's quite obvious that the dates in this zodiac correspond to the Western zodiac, and many of the signs share similar explanations and attributes. So it can be construed that Native animal symbols were used to create a Native American–style zodiac similar to the Western one. Many of the animals used in this zodiac also have different meanings to different peoples across North America.

Also, many descriptions of the animals in the zodiac contradict the natural lifestyle of the animal. For example, under the wolf sign, it is said wolves are fiercely independent while wolves themselves are social animals, living most of their lives in packs. There are positive and negative attributes to each zodiac animal as well.

So the Native American zodiac should not be considered the complete definition of animal symbols to Native people but just another piece of information further explaining the importance of spirit animals.

Otter
January 20 to February 18

Otters are considered unorthodox. They have an unusual way of looking at things, but often have quick minds and intelligence. "Quirky" is a fine term to describe otters. But they can be great friends because they are perceptive. They can be sensitive, courageous and honest. However, otters can also be lewd, rebellious and sneaky.

Wolf
February 19 to March 20

The wolf is fiercely independent, passionate and emotional. Wolves can be generous, deeply loving and gentle, but they also have a strong need for freedom and being alone. Wolves can be impractical, obsessive and vindictive.

Falcon
March 21 to April 19

Falcons are natural born leaders, never wasting their time, taking action when action needs to be taken. A bit conceited and arrogant at times, they are usually correct in their opinions. Falcons can be passionate and strong but also vain, intolerant and overly sensitive to criticism.

Beaver
April 20 to May 20

Beavers get the job done, efficiently and with aplomb. The beaver is all business, sometimes too much, but their mental abilities are made for work. Beavers are usually right, but sometimes they lack tact and diplomacy in their dealings with others. With the correct influence, beavers are compassionate, loyal and helpful. Unfortunately, they can also be arrogant, over-demanding and possessive.

Deer
May 21 to June 20

The deer is lively and quick-witted, able to get anyone to laugh. Deer love to talk and are great at it, having sparkly personalities. However, they have a tendency to focus too much on themselves. With the right influence, deer can be an inspiring force. They can also be selfish, moody, impatient and lazy.

Woodpecker
June 21 to July 21

Woodpeckers are extremely empathic, great listeners, perfect to have on your side as a friend or soul mate. Usually the most nurturing of all the Native American animal symbols, they also make great parents. Woodpeckers are caring, devoted and romantic. But woodpeckers can also be possessive, angry and jealous.

Salmon
July 22 to August 21

Full of energy, salmon are natural motivators, confident and enthusiastic. They have plenty of friends who are attracted to their intelligence and intuition. Positive aspects of the salmon include stability and calmness but with powerful energy. However, salmon can also be egotistical, rude and intolerant.

Bear
August 22 to September 21

The bear is usually the voice of reason, the person to call on when you need someone with a level head. Very practical, patient and tolerant, bears make great business partners or teachers and mentors. In a positive light, bears are modest and generous. But with a negative influence, bears can be skeptical, lazy and shy to the point of being reclusive.

Raven
September 22 to October 22

Ravens are highly enthusiastic, naturally charming with an easy energy. They make great entrepreneurs, and they are ingenious and idealistic. They can be patient, easygoing and intuitive. However, ravens can also be inconsistent, abrasive and demanding.

Snake
October 23 to November 22

Snakes make great spiritual leaders because they feel comfortable in the matters of the spirit. They also have great healing abilities but also have a desire to explore mysterious ideas that some may find dark. Snakes can be passionate, funny, helpful and inspiring. But they can also become secretive, depressed and preoccupied.

Owl
November 23 to December 21

The owl goes at life at full speed and is a lover of adventure and a friend to the world. Owls are great artists and teachers, but they are also so versatile that they can excel in almost anything they do.

Sometimes they can be reckless, but that just adds to the adventure. Owls can be sensitive, enthusiastic and attentive, but that can also turn to overindulgence, dangerous risk-taking and bitterness.

Goose
December 22 to January 19

The goose is ambitious, driven and always gets the job done. Geese are determined to succeed at all costs, which makes them excel in business or sports, among other endeavors. These characteristics also make for a passionate person who is funny and deeply driven to be with and to help others. However, this can also turn to obsessive behavior and the ignoring of loved ones in order to get the job done.

Notes on Sources

Book Sources

Alsop II, Fred J. *Birds of North America*. New York: Smithsonian Handbooks, 2001.

Beer, Amy-Jane, and Pat Morris. *Encyclopedia of North American Mammals*. San Diego, CA: Thunder Bay Press, 2004.

Bruchac, Joseph. *Our Stories Remember: American Indian History, Culture and Values Through Storytelling*. Golden, CO: Fulcrum Publishing, 2003.

Ching, Elise Dirlam, and Kaleo Ching. *Faces of the Soul: Rituals in Art Maskmaking and Guided Imagery*. Berkeley, CA: North Atlantic Books, 2006.

Dembicki, Matt (ed.). *Trickster: Native American Tales: A Graphic Collection*. Golden, CO: Fulcrum Books, 2010.

Eldrich, Lise. *Bears Make Rock Soup and Other Stories*. San Francisco, CA: Children's Book Press, 2002.

Farmer, Steven D. *Animal Spirit Guides*. Carlsbad, CA: Hay House, 2006.

Farmer, Steven D. *Power Animals*. Carlsbad, CA: Hay House Inc., 2004.

Flying with the Eagle, Racing the Great Bear: Tales From Native North America. Told by Joseph Bruchac. Golden CO: Fulcrum Publishing, 2011.

Gunn, Celia M. *Simply Totem Animals*. New York: Sterling/Zambezi, 2010.

Harmer, Lucy. *Discovering Your Spirit Animal*. Berkeley, CA: North Atlantic Books, 2009.

Jacobs, Alan. *Native America Wisdom*. London: Watkins Publishing, 2008.

Lake-Thom, Bobby. *Spirits of the Earth, A Guide to Native American Nature, Symbols, Stories and Ceremonies*. New York: Plume Books, 1997.

Martinez, David. *The Legends and Lands of Native North Americans*. New York: Sterling Publishing, 2003.

Nitsch, Twylah. *Creature Teachers: A Guide to the Spirit Animals of the Native America Tradition*. New York: Continuum, 2000.

Pippert, Dorothy, and Stephen J. Spignesi. *Native American History for Dummies*. Wiley Publishing, 2008.

Raczek, Linda. *Stories from Native North America*. Austin, TX: RSVP Books, 2000.

Ruppert, James, and John W. Bernet (eds.). *Our Voices: Native Stories of Alaska and the Yukon*. Toronto: University of Toronto Press, 2001.

Steige, Brad. *Totems: The Transformation Power of Your Personal Animal Totem*. New York: Harper Collins, 1997.

The Girl Who Helped Thunder and Other Native American Folktales. Retold by James Bruchac and Joseph Bruchac. New York: Sterling Publishing, 2008.

Thornhill, Jan. *Folktails: Animal Legends from Around the World*. Toronto, ON: Maple Tree Press, 1993.

Song, Tamarcak, and Beaver, Moses (Amik). *Whispers of the Ancients*. Michigan: University of Michigan Press, 2010.

Website Sources

http://esask.uregina.ca (the online encyclopedia of Saskatchewan)

www.indianmythology.org

www.mpm.edu/wirp/ICW-03.html (Ojibwa culture website)

www.muiniskw.org (website on Mik'maq culture)

www.native-languages.org

www.powwows.com

Credit: Maki Blazevski

Wayne Arthurson

Award-winning author Wayne Arthurson is an
Aboriginal freelance writer, who has written pro-
fessionally for over 20 years and has worked full
time as a journalist, editor, communications officer
and an advertising copywriter. He has more than
100 articles, five history books and three novels
already published, including *Fall from Grace*, winner of the Alberta Readers' Choice award. Wayne is
also the author of *In the Shadow of Our Ancestors* for
Eschia Books.